With the Compliments

of

Fred Hanna Ltd.

New & Second-hand Booksellers,
27-28-29 Nassau Street,
Dublin 2.

Recordmakers

OF GAELIC GAMES

Owen McCann

Oisín Publications

© Oisín Publications 1996
4 Iona Drive, Dublin 9.
Tel. 01-8305236/8309473. Fax: 8307860.

Oisín Publications wish to thank
Padraig O'Dea, Manager, A.I.B. Bank, Drumcondra
and Hugh Cawley, General Manager, A.I.B. Bank, Dublin,
for their support in the publication of this book.

Recordmakers is a tribute to the dedicated players
who devoted their time, energy and commitment
to establishing the outstanding records in Gaelic Games.

Table of Contents

Photographs

THE CURRENT DECADE

GOLDEN NINETIES FOR PETER CANAVAN

Peter Canavan has been associated with more record-making achievements than most during these early years of the 'Nineties.

The dashing forward led Tyrone to their first All-Ireland under-21 football title in 1991 when the O'Neill County men thrashed mighty Kerry by 4-16 to 1-5 at Newbridge. Canavan enhanced the achievement by scoring a majestic 2-5 before an attendance of 6,000.

Tyrone were again captained by Canavan in the 1992 campaign, and the county beat Galway by three points at Longford to retain the All-Ireland under-21 crown. Canavan became the first, and so far only man, to captain two national title winning teams in the grade.

He was again very much on the scoring target in the 1992 final. His return did not match his *tour-de-force* of the previous season's final, but he still finished the game against Galway

Peter Canavan ...
a place apart in under-21 football

1

with a splendid seven points.

Peter Canavan continued on the history-making trail in 1993 – and once again in the role of a successful captain. He led Errigal-Ciaran to victory over defending champions Moortown in August for a first-ever Tyrone senior football title.

Errigal Ciaran went on to capture the Ulster senior crown, and were only beaten by eventual champions, Nemo Rangers of Cork, in extra time in the All-Ireland semi-final at Newbridge.

That game was played on Saturday, March 5, 1994. The following afternoon Canavan went in from the substitutes' bench for Ulster against Munster in the Railway Cup final at Ennis. Eleven minutes after the interval, the Tyrone man put the final golden flourish to a sparkling Ulster movement by beating Peter O'Leary (Kerry) in the Southern goal for a history-making score.

That Canavan goal really clinched victory for Ulster by two points and with it ranking for the province as the first to win five interprovincial football titles in succession.

Special Place For Pascal Russell

Clare county senior hurling championship medals in three decades and the first to win four county senior medals with Clarecastle, that was the double distinction earned by Pascal Russell when as full forward he did much to fashion his club's six points win over Scarriff in the 1991 decider.

Russell won his first county senior medal in 1970 and collected two in the 'Eighties – 1986 and 1987. Then came that 1991 triumph to complete a remarkable run over such a lengthy period.

Noteworthy Goal

Eanna Ryan scored many vital goals during his career in senior hurling, but one of special significance was chalked up while assisting, not his native Galway, but the All-Stars.

Ryan lined out at right half forward for the All-Stars against Tipperary in the first hurling game at the Skydome in Toronto in 1990 and four minutes after the start found his way through to the Munster county net for the first of eight goals recorded during that game.

The Galway man finished with 2-2, but was beaten on the individual scoring chart by Nicholas English, who hit 2-4 for Tipperary, and who won by 5-15 to 3-11.

Dublin beat Tyrone in the first football game at the Skydome in 1990 and

Vinny Murphy scored the only goal of that game at the end of the third quarter. He lined out at centre half forward and finished with 1-1. Dublin won by 1-8 to 0-10.

RARE DOUBLE FOR MANUS BOYLE

Manus Boyle completed a rare scoring double when he finished Donegal's top scorer in their winning All-Ireland senior football final debut in 1992 against Dublin by rifling over nine points. Understandably, that is a peak for a Donegal man in a Sam Maguire Cup tie.

Five years earlier, Boyle scored 1-7 as Donegal beat Kerry in a replay at Roscommon for a second All-Ireland under-21 football title. That is the best individual score by a Donegal man in an All-Ireland final and Boyle finished the team's leading scorer in the 1987 campaign with 3-28 (37 points) in eight games.

HEADY DAYS FOR THE COLEMANS

Derry's memorable break-through in the All-Ireland senior football championship with that winning final debut in 1993 at Cork's expense, was an extra special day for Eamonn Coleman and his son, Gary.

Eamonn was manager of the side, and Gary held down the left half back position in the summit.

Both had enjoyed All-Ireland title winning success before Derry finally put their name on the Sam Maguire Cup.

As a player, Eamonn helped Derry to a couple of "Famous Firsts." He was left half forward in the side that beat Kerry in 1965 to bring the Tom Markham Cup for the All-Ireland minor football championship to Derry for the first time. Eamonn contributed two points on a day that also marked Derry's first appearance in an under-18 national summit.

Three years later, Coleman, in the No. 10 jersey, contributed a goal and many fine touches as Derry beat Offaly at Croke Park for a first All-Ireland under-21 final win.

Eamonn added an Ulster senior medal to his collection in 1970, but did not, of course, play in a Sam Maguire Cup tie. However, his name will still be linked in a prominent way with the never-to-be-forgotten triumph of 1993 over Cork as a result of his tremendous contribution behind the scenes as team manager.

Gary brought a second All-Ireland minor football medal to the family as a polished centre half back and captain in the side that beat Offaly in 1989.

He held down the left half back berth in the team that beat Tyrone in 1992 for

Derry's second National League title and completed a major national double at No. 7 in the Sam Maguire Cup triumph over Cork.

An interprovincial medal is now the only important trophy missing from Gary's collection.

BROWNE'S DOUBLE LINK

Colm Browne is linked in a special way with two major triumphs in the annals of Laois senior football. He was left half back in the team that beat Monaghan in 1986 for the first win by Laois in a National League final since beating Dublin in the inaugural final in 1927. Browne also captained the 1986 team.

In the autumn of 1993 he took over as county senior football team manager in Laois, and within weeks had guided the county to the All-Ireland senior football "B" title. A wonderful start to his then new position.

Denis Lalor led Laois to their final win over Sligo from midfield and became the first from the county to skipper an All-Ireland championship winning team since the junior football title triumph of 1973.

A FIRST FOR FERMANAGH

Peter Quinn became the first Fermanagh man to take over the Presidency of the G.A.A. in 1991, and went on to be linked in a special way with a truly golden era for Ulster football.

Quinn had only taken over the post when he presented Tony Scullion (Derry) with the interprovincial trophy as captain of the Ulster team that beat Munster in the then Iarnród Éireann final at Croke Park. Who would have been so bold then as to predict that the President from Fermanagh would go on to present the Sam Maguire Cup to three Northerners in succession?

That's exactly what happened, as Paddy O'Rourke (Down) in 1991, Anthony Molloy (Donegal) 1992, and Henry Downey (Derry) 1993, climbed the Hogan Stand steps after All-Ireland senior football final wins.

Quinn did not spare himself during his term as President. He travelled widely both at home and abroad, and guided the organisation wisely and well.

He will always be linked with the big development scheme at Croke Park, which he successfully got "off the ground" during his term in office.

Author Owen McCann and Peter Quinn photographed at the launch of
The Shell Book of the McCarthy Cup *at Croke Park*

THE NINETIES

TEDDY MCCARTHY – THE MAN OF THE DECADE

Teddy McCarthy, the gifted dual player from Glanmire, in Cork, must rank as the player of the current decade, after the unique manner in which he rang in the 'Nineties by winning All-Ireland senior championship medals in hurling and football in September 1990. He became the first-ever to win medals in both codes in the same year.

In these days, when competition is so keen in both games, it is an achievement for any player to win an All-Ireland senior medal in hurling or football. To win hurling and football souvenirs in the same month as a senior is the material of which fairy-tales are made.

Teddy McCarthy ... Legendary Achievement

McCarthy's legendary achievement was all the more meritorious for the fact that he came back from an ankle injury to complete the big double. The injury kept the Cork man out of both Munster finals in 1990, and it is a tribute to his bravery, dedication and skill that he battled back so well to earn a place apart in the annals of Gaelic Games.

Teddy made four appearances in hurling and two in football on the way to the great double. He was at left midfield in the side that beat Galway in hurling and left half forward in the football final triumph at the expense of Meath.

McCarthy had taken his place in the exclusive ranks of dual All-Ireland senior medalists before 1990. He was right half forward in the 1986 All-Ireland senior hurling title winning team. Then in 1989 he became the fifteenth player to gain medals in both codes, following his appearance at centrefield in the football final win over Mayo.

However, his great double in 1990 was well out of the ordinary and the odds on any player equalling that feat before the end of the decade, or even longer, must be great indeed.

The trend in the dual medalists rankings was set early on by William J Spain, a native of Nenagh. He was in the Limerick Commercials side that won the football final of 1887, the very first in the history of the All-Ireland series. He helped Kickhams, of Dublin, to collect the 1889 hurling crown.

William Mackessy won medals with Cork in hurling in 1903 and in football in 1911 to become the first to win both awards with his native county.

Pierce Grace, a native of Tullaroan, Kilkenny, was in the Dublin teams that won the 1906 and 1907 football titles. He helped Kilkenny to their hurling triumphs of 1911, 1912 and 1913.

Spain and Grace alone won medals with different counties.

Wexford won their initial hurling crown in 1910 and their selection included PJ Mackey and Seán O'Kennedy.

Both were in the county's senior football title winning teams of 1915, 1916 and 1917. Mackey was also in action with Wexford in 1918 when the Model County footballers recorded the first run of four All-Ireland senior titles in succession by any county in the code.

Frank Burke, a native of Kildare, joined the elite by winning medals with Dublin in 1917 and 1920 (hurling) and 1921, 1922 and 1923 (football).

Leonard McGrath was twice "in" on history as he took his place in the exclusive company. He helped Galway to a first hurling title in 1923, and was in action with the side that won the county's first football crown two seasons later.

After McGrath's double there was a long lapse until the 'Forties, the decade when Cork hurling blossomed so brilliantly that the county marched to the only run of four All-Ireland senior championships in succession in the code. Cork achieved that unique feat from 1941 to 1944, inclusive.

Jack Lynch, who later became Taoiseach, played in all four hurling title winning teams. A year later he helped Cork to their first All-Ireland senior football title in 34 years and also the first Sam Maguire Cup triumph ever by a Leeside combination. In 1946 he won a fifth hurling medal.

As a result, Lynch became the only man to play in six senior title-winning combinations in succession.

Derry Beckett was also in the 1942 All-Ireland senior hurling title winning team and won a football medal in 1945.

MEMORABLE DECADE

Then came the memorable decade that was the 'Seventies. It was Cork all the way yet again, starting with the Liam McCarthy Cup triumph of 1970 at the expense of Wexford.

Ray Cummins was Cork's full forward in that hurling final win, the first 80 minutes decider. He was also at full forward when the footballers regained the Sam Maguire Cup by outscoring Galway in 1973.

Cork's football team that year also included Brian Murphy, left full back, Denis Coughlan, midfield, and Jimmy Barry-Murphy, right full forward.

Murphy at right full back, Coughlan at left half back, and left half forward Barry-Murphy took their places in the exclusive company of dual medallists following the 1976 win by Cork over Wexford hurlers.

Cummins also won another medal in 1976 – he was captain that year – and also played in the 1977 and 1978 hurling title winning sides. Murphy, Coughlan and Barry-Murphy were also in the two latter teams.

Barry-Murphy collected further medals in 1984 and 1986.

Liam Currams was midfielder in the Offaly team that won the All-Ireland senior hurling crown for the first time in 1981. A year later he was at left half back as Offaly, with a sensational late, late goal, ended Kerry's ambitions on the post of a record-making run of five All-Ireland senior football titles in succession.

Then came Teddy McCarthy's double in 1986 and 1989 to march on in 1990 to that extra special place in this most select company of All-Ireland senior medal winners.

*Ray Cummins with upraised hurley on the way to another
All-Ireland medal as Cork's captain in 1976*

DOWN THE YEARS

TWO GAMES WITH TWO CLUBS ON SAME DAY

It is not unusual for a footballer or hurler to play two games on the same afternoon, but not many can point to having appeared with two separate clubs in competitive fare on the same day – and legally at that!

Tom Long, who won All-Ireland senior football medals with Kerry in 1959 and 1962, and Brendan Keane (Mayo) earned such a rare distinction back in March 1957.

They were team-mates with Erin's Hope, the Student Teacher team attached to St Patrick's Training College at Drumcondra, in a 1956 Dublin Senior Football League game against Na Fianna at Balbriggan in 1957.

Immediately following the final whistle, Long and Keane changed into the jerseys of Clan na Gael and played against St Vincent's in a Senior Football League tie. They were on the winning side in each match.

The pair were eligible to play for Clan na Gael because both were then members of the club, having finished their term at the Training College. As they had played for Erin's Hope in some of the 1956 League games before leaving the College, they were eligible to finish out that competition with the College.

SHARPSHOOTING POTTERTON

Meath blazed an impressive trail in hurling in 1993 by capturing the All-Ireland "B" championship for the first time. A bright feature of the success story was the lethal finishing of Pat Potterton.

The dynamic left midfielder found the target in great style. He scored a superb 0-38 over the four game march to the title and that earned him a majestic match average of 9.50 points.

Potterton scored in every game, and chalked up his best match return against Derry in a semi-final at Keady,where he rifled over twelve points.

The win earned Meath a place in the All-Ireland quarter-final against Antrim. They lost that game at Castleblayney, but still put up an encouraging performance, and, all in all, the Royal County – and Potterton – helped to brighten the 1993 hurling year in a big way.

DIAMOND WALKS INTO HISTORY

Tommy Diamond captained the Derry team that won the All-Ireland under-21 football title in 1968 by beating Offaly at Croke Park – and promptly walked into history on two counts.

That was the initial final by an Ulster team – indeed the first-ever appearance by a Northern county in an under-21 national summit. Diamond played at right half back, and earned ranking as the first to captain All-Ireland minor and under-21 football title winning teams.

Three years earlier he led Derry from midfield when they made an historic break-through by beating Kerry to join the ranks of All-Ireland minor championship winners for the first time.

O'LEARY – A SPECIAL GOALKEEPER

John O'Leary, who has given a tremendous service to Dublin in goal since 1980, earned a special niche for himself in the county's 1992-93 National Football League title win. He captained the side – the first goalkeeper to gain such an honour with the Dubs.

O'Leary, who had won League medals earlier in 1987 and 1991, played in every one of the 11 games contested by Dublin on the way to their eighth title.

The Dubliner is a member of O'Dwyer's, Balbriggan, and plays outfield with his club.

John O'Leary, securely in possession for Dublin, and the first goalkeeper to lead the county to a League title.

POWER FORCE

Top medal wins at home and abroad earned Bill Carlos a proud place among the record-makers in Gaelic Games. He was the first to figure in an All-Ireland senior title winning side, the victorious team in a New York v "Home," winners in a National League final proper, and a successful St Brendan's Cup winning XV. Carlos was an inspiring centre half back for Roscommon in their only Sam Maguire Cup winning sides of 1943 and 1944. Later he went to New York and helped the Exiles record a sensational win over Cavan in 1950 at Croke Park. That game marked New York's debut in a League summit, and Carlos became the only native of the county so far to win All-Ireland senior and League medals.

After 1952, New York's League connection ended for a time. A new series for the St Brendan Cup was inaugurated in 1954 between the League champions and New York, and the Exiles, with Carlos included, beat Mayo at the Polo Grounds.

ONLY TWO FOR DERRY

Séamus Downey bridged a long, long gap for Derry when he goaled against Cork after fourteen and a half minutes in the 1993 All-Ireland senior football final. That was only the second goal scored by a Derry man for his native county in a Sam Maguire Cup tie.

Full forward Owen Gribben hit Derry's only goal ten minutes into the second half of their All-Ireland senior final debut in 1958 against Dublin. Derry had to wait until 1993 for their next final appearance.

Enda Gormley was top scorer for the Northerners in the 1993 game with 0-6, three points from frees, and that ranks as the best score by a Derry man in a Sam Maguire Cup match.

CENTENARY MEN

Joe Cassells, who took over the captaincy of the Meath senior football team for the 1988 All-Ireland senior football final replay after missing most of the earlier games because of injury, was in a sense repeating history.

Mick Lyons captained Meath in the drawn final of 1988 against Cork, and Cassells went into that game as a substitute. He retained his place for the replay and led Meath to a successful defence of the title.

Back in the GAA Centenary Year of 1984, the Association promoted Ford Centenary Cup competitions in football and hurling as part of the celebrations.

Cassells was outstanding at centre half back for Meath in their final win over Monaghan at Croke Park in 1984. He took over the role as team leader after

Eamonn Barry, Meath captain at the time, had to miss the final because of an ankle injury he picked up on the previous Sunday in a Centenary Cup semi-final against Cavan at Croke Park. He lined out in that game at centre half forward.

The Centenary Cup final was Meath's first major top title win following the League title success of 1975. Joe Cassells was a member of that team.

John Fenton has more cause than most to remember the Centenary Year. He led Munster to their Railway Cup final win over Leinster at Ennis on March 18, the day the Centenary Year was launched.

Fenton skippered Cork to their Centenary Cup final win over Laois at Croke Park and hit five points. Then, in September, he skippered the Rebel County to victory over Offaly in the All-Ireland senior final played at Semple Stadium, Thurles.

Joe Cassells ...
Centenary captain with Meath

EGAN SCORES FOR CORK – AT LAST!

Barry Egan did more than finish as the country's leading scorer for the 1992-93 National Hurling League with his splendid return of 3-44 (53) points in twelve games, at an average of 4.41 points a match. He became the first Cork hurler to head the national chart in a full Hurling League season since I introduced these particular charts in 1964-65.

Cork beat Wexford in the final after two replays to regain the title after a twelve year interval. At the end of 1993, Egan completed a big double by joining the ranks of Bank of Ireland All Stars award winners with his selection at left full forward.

HORAN AGAIN

Pádraig Horan was manager of the Offaly team that won the National Hurling League for the first time in 1990-91. As a result, he commands a special place with a double first for the Faithful County. He led Offaly from full foward to their initial Liam McCarthy Cup triumph in 1981 at the expense of the then defending champions, Galway.

HISTORIC SCORE

At a time when Dublin are struggling so hard to make a worthwhile impression in any grade of inter-county hurling, it is interesting to record an extra special score by a Dubliner in a major competitive game.

Dublin and Wexford clashed in a Leinster under-21 semi-final in 1967 at Kilkenny. Less than a minute from time Eugene Davey, wearing the No. 11 jersey, goaled for the Dubs. It was also an historic score as it knocked Wexford out of the provincial championship for the first time. The Slaneysiders contested the inaugural All-Ireland final of 1964, and won the title a year later. They lost the 1966 All-Ireland final to Cork, after two replays.

A DERRY MAN ON HIS OWN

Henry Downey naturally enough earned a special place in the annals of Derry football when he led the Oak Leafcounty to their first All-Ireland senior football final win in 1993. The win over Cork provided another chapter in setting the Lavey man apart in Derry football.

In 1992, he was right half back and captain in the side that beat Tyrone in the Royal Liver National League Final at Croke Park, thanks in the main to a late, late goal from a "45" by towering midfielder Anthony Tohill.

That was not Derry's first League title – they won a restricted competition in 1947. However, the Sam Maguire Cup triumph completed a double for Downey to leave him the only man to captain the county to National League and All-Ireland senior final wins.

Incidentally, Downey first appeared in inter-county competitions as a hurler. He joined the county senior football team on a regular basis in 1991. He was in the Lavey team that won the All-Ireland club senior football crown for the only time in 1991.

14

RARE TREBLE FOR ANTHONY MOLLOY

Anthony Molloy completed a rare treble as a county team captain when he led Donegal to victory over Clare in the 1992-93 National Football League semi-final at Croke Park in April 1993.

He was captain when Donegal beat Mayo in a 1992 All-Ireland senior football championship semi-final – the North-West county's first senior championship win at Croke Park. Molloy led Donegal to victory over the Dublin side in September in the All-Ireland senior final.

Anthony Molloy ... completed a rare treble as Donegal captain. He is photographed with his wife, Breige, and Terry Taylor, left, Regional Sales Manager, Bass, Ireland

Then came the 1-12 to 1-7 win over Clare and with it a first-ever triumph by Donegal in a National League semi-final.

Molloy's hopes of making it a clean sweep of "Famous Firsts" were dashed by Dublin in a replay in the League summit.

The Donegal man was in a sense again "walking in history" during those heady days for the North-West county. He was a powerful unit at midfield with Donal Reid in the under-21 team that beat Roscommon by 0-8 to 0-5 at Carrick-on-Shannon in 1982 to capture the county's first All-Ireland championship proper.

Donegal was captained in that game by Brian Tuohy, from Aodh Rua, Ballyshannon, who played at left half back.

WANTED – BY TWO PROVINCES!

Paul Russell, of Kerry, helped an all-Kerry Munster selection beat Connacht in the inaugural Railway Cup football final in 1927. He was chosen for the 1928 competition by both Munster and Leinster.

Russell, who was a Dublin representative in 1928, played with Leinster after a Central Council ruling, and proved a hero of the final win over Ulster.

Playing at half back, Russell scored three long range points in the last few minutes to snatch a dramatic one point win.

So, Russell won a medal in the first final when representing Munster, and a year later helped Leinster to their first title ... a remarkable record-making double.

Incidentally, Paul Russell was only 17 when he was chosen for Kerry for the 1923 All-Ireland senior final. A splendid achievement that, but that is still not the full story!

Russell had not played for Kerry in any grade prior to his call-up to the senior team, nor had he taken part in any trial game!

UNDER-21 SKIPPER

Leitrim's captain in their first Connacht under-21 football final win in 1977 was Frank Holohan. He was centre half back in the side that beat Roscommon at Sligo in the decider.

Holohan was in the Leitrim team that finished runners-up for the 1972 All-Ireland Vocational Schools championship. He played club football with Drumreilly.

CAPTAINS APART

Tony Scullion (Derry), Peter Finnerty (Galway) and Danny Owens (Offaly) walked together in history as title winning captains in 1991.

The old Railway Cup interprovincial competitions were replaced that year by a new series known as the Iarnród Éireann Cups. Scullion and Finnerty captained Ulster footballers and Connacht hurlers to final wins over Munster in each code.

Owens led Offaly into the National Hurling League record books as they emerged from Division II in 1990-91 to surprise fancied Wexford in the final at Croke Park and capture the title for the first time.

Owens held down the right full forward position and (appropriately enough!) also headed the county's scoring chart for the entire campaign with 2-42 (48 points) from nine appearances at an average of 5.33 points a match.

Scoring Giants

Matt Connor – Record Maker Extraordinary

Many footballers and hurlers have down the years graced Gaelic Games with their extra special skills and polished techniques in consistently chalking up the scores. Forwards, with the ability and flair to regularly colour matches with noteworthy individual scoring returns, command prominent positions in the nation-wide scoring charts over lengthy periods.

Matt Connor ...
Sharpshooter
Supreme

Matt Connor proved a supreme artist in this regard in a comparatively short inter-county senior career in football. He found the target in a manner unequalled by probably any other footballer or hurler in the long history of the national games.

He made his senior inter-county debut with Offaly in a National League game at Tullamore in March 1978, and really "arrived" as a rich jewel among the scoring wizards in 1980.

That year, the Walsh Island club man became the first in football or hurling to reach 200 points, goals and points combined, in a full annual campaign. Connor scored 22 goals and 135 points (201 points) in 29 games and no footballer has reached even 190 points in the meantime.

A year later, Connor was again very target conscious, finishing the season with a splendid 16-140 (188 points) in 30 games. Not unexpectedly, the Offaly man was the leading scorer in the country in 1980 and 1981. He retained that position in 1982, 1983 and 1984, and is the only player to command such a proud role over five seasons in succession.

The Offaly man is also the only man to head the annual review over five annual programmes. His goals tally of 22 in 1980 is also a record for a year's series, and his 140 points in 1981 is also the best in this regard.

So, Matt Connor ranks indeed as a record-maker extraordinary. His brilliant career was ended prematurely as a result of a serious car accident on Christmas Day, 1984.

Paddy Doherty headed the football table for the first time in 1960 and his tally of 13-97 (136 points) in 24 games still ranks as the tops for an Ulster footballer.

Mick O'Dwyer scored 13 goals and 122 points in 26 games in 1970 for what ranks as the record by a Munster player. His total includes 9-30 (57 points) in seven games on Kerry's World Tour in March, which took in five games in Australia, one in Auckland, New Zealand, and one in San Francisco.

Michael Kearins, probably Sligo's greatest ever footballer, holds the record for a Connacht player at 4-103 (145 points) in 19 games in 1972.

KEHER ON HIS OWN

Eddie Keher in a class of his own in scoring records

Eddie Keher was in a class all his own in hurling when it came to sending home the goals and points with rare abandon. He was the nation's top scorer ten years outright between 1965 and 1976, and shared the lead spot on his debut in 1963 with Jimmy Doyle (Tipperary).

Between 1963 and 1976, he was out of the top two nationally only once – in 1964.

In addition, he holds sway on top of the chart of annual returns in hurling, with a staggering 194 points (20-134) in only 21 games in 1972. A year earlier, he scored 8-141 (165 points) in 17 games to establish a new peak for the code at that time.

Eddie Keher stepped up to the senior ranks in 1959, and went close to 300 appearances in the premier grade. He bowed out of senior inter-county competitions following a challenge game against old rivals Wexford at Enniscorthy in August 1977, in which he scored three points.

That scoreline brought his record over all to a superb 211 goals and 1,426 (2,059 points) from 298 games.

A sharpshooter of exceptional class – that was Eddie Keher.

Nick Rackard was the first "Century-Maker" in hurling in 1956. The dynamic Wexford forward hit 35 goals and 50 points (155 points) in 19 games. His goals tally ranks as the best in the code for an annual programme.

Joe Connolly became the first Galway hurler to pass out the "Ton Up" marker with a scoreline of 5-87 (102 points) in 20 games in 1980. However, that was still only good enough to earn him second place nationally, six points adrift of Eamonn Cregan (Limerick).

PJ Molloy passed out the century in 1982 and also established a new record for a Galway – and Connacht – hurler as he led the way country-wide with 15-91 (136 points) from 20 games. This remains the standard which forwards from the West have to aim at as the provincial record.

Special mention must be made of the achievement of David Kilcoyne in leading the way in 1984 with 16-97 (145 points) in 20 games. A tremendous feat, that, for any hurler but all the more creditable for Kilcoyne as his county, Westmeath, is not one of the leading lights of the sport.

LEADING ANNUAL RETURNS

The outstanding returns in annual campaigns in football and hurling for all games, league, championship, challenge, interprovincial and representative matches are:

FOOTBALL

POINTS		SCORE	GAME	YEAR
201	Matt Connor (Offaly)	22-135	29	1980
188	Matt Connor (Offaly)	16-140	30	1981
161	Mick O'Dwyer (Kerry)	13-122	26	1970
150	Matt Connor (Offaly)	13-111	25	1984
145	Matt Connor (Offaly)	14-103	24	1983
142	Michael Kearins (Sligo)	4-130	19	1972
141	Michael Kearins (Sligo)	2-135	24	1968
136	Paddy Doherty (Down)	13-97	24	1960

HURLING

POINTS		SCORE	GAME	YEAR
194	Eddie Keher (Kilkenny)	20-134	21	1972
165	Eddie Keher (Kilkenny	8-141	17	1971
155	Nick Rackard (Wexford)	35-50	19	1956
145	David Kilcoyne (Westmeath)	16-97	20	1984
141	Eddie Keher (Kilkenny)	18-87	16	1975
139	Eddie Keher (Kilkenny)	12-103	17	1974
138	Eddie Keher (Kilkenny)	20-78	18	1976
136	PJ Molloy (Galway)	15-91	20	1982

FOOTBALL CHAMPIONSHIP

BRIAN STAFFORD SHOOTS
TO A NEW HIGH

The Senior Football Championship season of 1991 was memorable for a gripping four game marathon featuring Meath and Dublin in a first round Leinster match. As the clock ticked relentlessly to the final seconds in the fourth game, Dublin looked poised for a place in the second round as they led by three points.

Then Meath defender Martin O'Connell started a movement along his own end line at the Canal end. Eleven Meath players were involved before defender Kevin Foley popped up in the Dublin defence to score his first-ever goal for the county.

David Beggy put the final finish to an exciting and wonderful series of games by sending over the last gasp winning point for Meath.

The sharpshooting of Brian Stafford was one of the most noteworthy aspects of the four game series. He chalked up a splendid 2-25 (31 points) and that was to help him in a big way along the road to a new record for the Senior Football Championship.

Meath reached the All-Ireland final, in which they lost to Down. They played ten games and full forward Stafford proved so target conscious that he finished the campaign with 74 points – 4-62 at an average of 7.40 points a game.

That well and truly passed out the old record set by Matt Connor (Offaly) in 1980 at 5-31 (46 points). However, as the Midlander only played four games, he still commands the top match average among the annual chart-toppers at a thundering 11.50 points a match.

Stafford scored in every game on the way to the new peak, and had his best match return at 0-10, seven points from frees, in the third encounter with Dublin, which went to extra time.

Incidentally, Meath played all their games in 1991 at Croke Park, and two of the stirring four matches against the Dubs went to extra time.

Stafford headed the annual table in 1991 for the second time that season. He made his entry in 1988 with 0-38 in five games, at an average of 7.60 points a match. He was back again in 1990 with 1-24, again in five games, for an average of 5.40 points.

The Meath man's points tally in 1991 is not unexpectedly the tops for an annual campaign.

Leading the way in the goals stakes are Michael Sheehy (Kerry) and Barney Rock (Dublin), with six each.

Sheehy, surprisingly enough, became Kerry's first representative in the annual returns as late as 1976, when he joined the ranks with 4-26 (38 points) in five games, at an average of 7.60 points a match. Three years later, he topped the table for the only other time, with 6-18 (36 points) in four outings at nine points a match.

Barney Rock joined the exclusive company of sharpshooters in 1983 with 6-26 (44 points) in seven games, or 6.28 points a match on average. He retained the top spot in 1984 and again in 1985.

Colin Corkery set a new standard for Munster in 1993 when he won his first

Brian Stafford ... new high in championship

ranking in the review on 3-31 (40 points) in five games, at an average of eight points a game. He became only the second Cork footballer to top an annual chart.

Tony McTague (Offaly), who helped the Midland County to a first Sam Maguire Cup win in 1971 and was in sharpshooting form again when they retained the trophy the following September, is the only footballer to head an annual table outright over four separate seasons.

He made his entry in 1969 with 1-34 (37 points) in six games, at an average of 6.16 points. The Midlander was back to dominate the chart in 1971, 1972 and 1973.

Jimmy Keaveney filled the leading spot over four campaigns as well, but in one season, 1977, he shared the rating with Dermot Earley (Roscommon). The Dubliner had his most successful season in 1975 with 1-38 (41 points) in five games, at an average of 8.20 points a game.

Hurling Championship

Eddie Keher Still Sets Pace

It is an indication of Eddie Keher's extra special qualities as an accurate finisher that, although he retired from inter-county hurling in 1977, he is still out on his own as far as major scoring achievements are concerned in the senior championship.

The dynamic Kilkenny stylist headed the annual chart for a full season's programme over four separate campaigns outright. He also shared the top spot once, and this record is the best by any hurler.

Keher not only holds the record score for a yearly programme, but also takes second place in this particular chart.

He made his entry into the ranks in 1963 with what was to prove his lowest annual scoreline at 2-25 (31 points) in three games, at an average of 10.33 points a match.

Eight seasons were to pass before Keher regained the leading position in the annual review. It proved a record-making come-back, as he bettered the then long standing record by four points.

Nick Rackard (Wexford) had set the marker with a thundering 12-15 (51 points) in only four games, at the wonderful match average of 12.75 points an outing. Keher carded 4-43 (55 points) in 1971, and as he, too, took only four games to reach that marker, he also bettered Rackard's match average at a majestic 13.75 points a game.

That remains the top match rating by any chart-topper for an annual programme.

Eddie Keher was in even sharpshooting form in 1972. Granted, his match average was somewhat down on the previous year, but he still rifled home a superb 6-45 (63 points) in five games. That worked out at a superb 12.60 points a game on average.

The Kilkenny man headed the country-wide table outright for the last time in 1974, but was back the following season to share the leading spot with Barney Moylan on 35 points. He scored 4-23 in three games, or 11.66 points a tie on average.

The only hurler other than Keher to fill the premier position outright over four campaigns is Jimmy Doyle (Tipperary), who led the way in 1960, 1961, 1962 and 1964.

Setting the standard for Munster is another Tipperary man, Pat Fox, who blazed an impressive trail in 1987 with 3-45 (54 points) in six games or nine points a match on average.

Joe Cooney brought Connacht – and Galway – in "out of the cold" as recently as 1990, by showing the other sharpshooters the way, with 1-24 in only three games at the very good match rating of nine points. He remains the only Westerner to fill such a position.

The late, great Nick Rackard set the goal standard as far back as 1956 with that impressive haul of twelve. No hurler has reached double figures in the goals review since then. Away ahead on the points review are Keher and Fox.

Keher set the pace with 45 in that record-making run of 1972, and Fox equalled that tally when he set the new record for the South in 1987.

DJ Carey joined the ranks of annual chart leaders in 1992, and retained that position a year later. He became the first hurler to top the chart two years in succession since Nicholas English (Tipperary) in 1988 and 1989.

ANNUAL RETURNS

The following are the leading annual returns in football and hurling in senior championship play.

FOOTBALL

74 points: Brian Stafford (Meath): 4-62 in ten games in 1991.
Average: 7.40 points.
46 points: Matt Connor (Offaly): 5-31 in four games in 1980.
Average: 11.50 points.
44 points: Barney Rock (Dublin): 6-26 in seven games in 1983.
Average 6.28 points.
42 points: Charlie Redmond (Dublin): 4-30 in six games in 1994.
Average: 7.00 points.
41 points: Peter Canavan (Tyrone) 1-38 in five games in 1995.
Average: 8.20 points.
41 points: Jimmy Keaveney (Dublin): 1-38 in five games in 1975.
Average: 8.20 points.
40 points: Colin Corkery (Cork): 3.31 in five games in 1993.
Average: 8.00 points.
39 points: Jimmy Keaveney (Dublin): 1-36 in six games in 1974.
Average: 6.50 points.

39 points: Barney Rock (Dublin): 5-24 in five games in 1984.
Average: 7.80 points
38 points: Charlie Gallagher (Cavan): 3-29 in five games in 1965.
Average: 7.60 points.
38 points: Tony McTague (Offaly): 1-35 in five games in 1971.
Average: 7.60 points.
38 points: Michael Sheehy (Kerry): 4-26 in five games in 1976.
Average: 7.60 points.
38 points: Larry Tompkins (Cork): 0-38 in six games in 1987.
Average: 6.33 points.
38 points: Brian Stafford (Meath): 0-38 in five games in 1988.
Average: 7.60 points.

HURLING

63 points: Eddie Keher (Kilkenny): 6-45 in five games in 1972.
Average 12.60 points.
55 points: Eddie Keher (Kilkenny): 4-43 in four games in 1971.
Average: 13.75 points.
54 points: Pat Fox (Tipperary): 3-45 in six games.
Average: 9 points.
51 points: Nick Rackard (Wexford): 12-15 in four games in 1956.
Average: 12.75 points.
50 points: Eddie Keher (Kilkenny): 5-35 in four games in 1974.
Average: 12.50 points.
50 points: Nicholas English (Tipperary): 4-38 in four games in 1989.
Average: 12.50 points.
45 points: Gary Kirby (Limerick): 4-33 in five games in 1994.
Average: 9 points.
41 points: DJ Carey (Kilkenny): 6-23 in six games in 1993.
Average: 6.83 points.
39 points: Paddy Molloy (Offaly): 8-15 in three games in 1969.
Average: 13.00 points.
39 points: Charlie McCarthy (Cork): 7-18 in five games in 1969.
Average: 7.80 points.
36 points: Jimmy Doyle (Tipperary): 4-24 in four games in 1960.
Average: 9 points.
36 points: John Fenton (Cork): 1-33 in four games in 1984.
Average: 9 points.
36 points: Jimmy Doyle (Tipperary): 6-18 in four games in 1960.
Average: 9 points.

Special Place For Canavan

Peter Canavan earned a special place in the ranks of top scorers in All-Ireland senior football finals when he helped himself to 0-11 for Tyrone in their unsuccessful bid against Dublin in the 1995 Bank of Ireland decider. This ranks as the leading individual return by a player on a losing side in football since I introduced these top scoring charts in 1955.

Jimmy Keaveney (Dublin) and Michael Sheehy (Kerry) share the record in football in a Sam Maguire Cup tie with 2-6 each.

Keaveney took over on top of the chart when he scored 2-6 against Armagh in his team's successful defence of the trophy in 1977. Previous to that, Frankie Stockwell dominated the chart with 2-5 for Galway in their 1956 final win over Cork. That still ranks as the leading return for a 60 minutes final. Keaveney reached his total in a 70 minutes game.

Sheehy joined the Dubliner on top of the table in 1979 when he did much to fashion Kerry's win over the Dubs in the second success in their sequence of four All-Ireland titles in succession.

Eoin Liston scored 3-2 for Kerry in 1978 against Dublin for the best goal return among the table toppers.

English Out In Front

Nicholas English raced impressively to the top of the hurling table when he did much to orchestrate Tipperary's win over Antrim in 1989 by scoring a superb 2-12.

He went clear of Eddie Keher, the great and legendary Kilkenny man, who, until then, had dominated the table with the leading four positions and a share of the then fifth spot with Eamonn Cregan (Limerick).

The leading scores in All-Ireland senior finals since 1955 are:

HURLING

POINTS	SCORE		YEAR
18	2-12	N. English (Tipperary) v. Antrim	1989
17	2-11	E. Keher (Kilkenny) v. Tipperary	1971
15	2-9	E. Keher (Kilkenny) v. Cork	1972
14	0-14	E. Keher (Kilkenny) v. Waterford	1963
	1-11	E. Keher (Kilkenny) v. Limerick	1974
13	2-7	E. Keher (Kilkenny) v. Galway	1975
	2-7	E. Cregan (Limerick) v. Galway	1980

| 12 | 1-9 | C. McCarthy (Cork) v. Wexford | 1970 |
| 11 | 3-2 | J. Keane (Waterford) v. Dublin | 1948 |

FOOTBALL

Points	Score		Year
12	2-6	J. Keaveney (Dublin) v. Armagh1	1977
	2-6	M. Sheehy (Kerry) v. Dublin	1979
11	3-2	E. Liston (Kerry) v. Dublin	1978
	2-5	F. Stockwell (Galway) v. Cork	1956
	0-11	P. Canavan (Tyrone) v. Dublin	1995
10	0-10	M. Fay (Meath) v. Kerry	1970
	0-10	A. McTague (Offaly) v. Kerry, Replay	1972
	1-7	B. Lynch (Kerry) v. Offaly, Draw	1972
9	1-6	M. Sheehy (Kerry) v. Roscommon	1980
	1-6	B. Rock (Dublin) v. Galway	1983
	0-9	C. Dunne (Galway) v. Kerry	1964
	2-3	S. Leydon (Galway) v. Offaly	1971
	0-9	J. Keaveney (Dublin) v. Galway	1974
	0-9	M. Boyle (Donegal) v. Dublin	1992

*Michael Sheehy (Kerry),
joint top scorer*

National Leagues – Football

Ger Heavin
New Prince Of The Sharpshooters

Ger Heavin blazed a brilliant new scoring trail during the 1993-94 season, to finish the leading marksman in the country. He made nine appearances with Westmeath in Division IV in a march to the quarter-finals, was in the side that then shocked Derry at Enniskillen, and bowed out of the series after a gallant failure to Meath.

Heavin helped himself to a majestic 7-58 (79 points) in eleven games at an average of 7.18 points a match. He well and truly left in tatters the old and fairly long-established record established by Tony McTague (Offaly) in 1971-72. He rifled over 0-66 that season in nine appearances at an average just fractionally above Heavin's at 7.33 points.

Heavin is the only Westmeath man to head an annual chart country-wide in football. He scored in every appearance and had his best match return against London at Castletown Geoghedan in November 1993 at 2-7. Both goals were from penalty kicks.

McTague's best match return in his record-setting season was against Mayo at Croke Park in March 1972, at 0-14. He was in immaculate shooting form in that game, in which he had fourteen shots at goal from free-kicks from all angles.

The Offaly marksman pointed eleven of the frees and put over a further brace of points from 'Fifties. So, he had just one miss and, for good measure, he notched a point from play as well.

Incidentally, his last point tied a memorable game. Coming up to the end, McTague faced up to a kick some 30 yards out at an angle to the right of the Railway goal … the last kick of the game. It was a test of nerve as well as skill of the kicker, but the ice-cool and deadly accurate McTague was not found wanting. He unerringly slotted the ball over the bar to earn Offaly a draw.

The closest any forward came to that McTague annual marker, until Heavin went a-score-taking in such exciting style, was in 1989-90, when Brian Stafford narrowly failed to equal the standard. The mighty scoring ace from Meath hit 7-44 (65 points) but, as he played twelve games, his match average was well down on McTague's at 5.41 points.

Tony McTague still holds one record in the League. He retained the top spot in the chart in 1972-73 and ranks as the only footballer to dominate the table over two seasons in succession.

Michael Kearins, undoubtedly Sligo's greatest-ever chance-snapper, went close to the McTague peak when he finished the 1973-74 season on top of the national chart with 0-64 in nine games, at an average well up on the Offaly man's in his big year, at 7.11 points a match.

Ger Heavin ... bright newcomer

The record for an Ulster footballer is 4-41 (53 points) by Ronan Carolan (Cavan) in eight games in 1991-92, at an average of 6.62 points a match.

The Munster standard is now the oldest in the chart, at 3-42 (51 points) by Mick O'Dwyer in 8 appearances with Kerry in 1969-70.

Although Tony McTague is the only footballer to head the national chart outright over two seasons in succession, Michael Kearins, Jimmy Keaveney (Dublin), Matt Connor (Offaly), Barney Rock (Dublin) and Brian Stafford also led the review out-right more than once.

Kearins is out

on his own in this regard, as he was the top marksman in 1967-68, 1970-71 and 1973-74. Keaveney's chart-leading years were 1974-75 and 1976-77. Connor was the ace scorer in 1981-82 and 1983-84.

Rock joined the ranks in 1985-86 and was back on top in 1988-89.

Stafford took his place for the first time in 1987-88 and then came that so-close bid to join McTague in a record-making role in 1989-90.

McTague's only appearances in the review was the record-making double run of the early 'Seventies.

Matt Connor shared a top of the table ranking with Stephen Joyce (Galway) in 1983-84. He scored 3-34 (43 points) in nine games and Joyce hit 1-40 in eleven games.

Barney Rock . . . joined ranks in 1985-86

National Leagues – Hurling

Keher, Hennessy – the 90 points plus marksmen

Eddie Keher, who chalked up the scores with remarkable fluency during a 22 years senior inter-county career with Kilkenny, and John Hennessy, of Kerry (yes, Kerry) rank as the only forwards in either code to have passed out 80 points in an annual campaign in the National League.

Keher and Hennessy did much better than that, in fact. The Kilkenny stylist proved so target conscious in 1975-76 that he swept to the top of the country-wide chart for that season with a resounding 11-59 (92 points) in eleven games, at an average of 8.36 points a game.

Keher scored on every appearance and he put up his best match return of the series at 3-3 in a drawn semi-final with Cork at Semple Stadium, Thurles, in April 1976.

That was to prove his final season as the leader in an annual nationwide review in the League and his fourth time to fill such a role. He led the way for the first time in 1966-67, with a then new record of 6-48 (66 points) in seven games, at his best match average in the top role in a season as leader, with 9.42 points a game. He returned to the No. 1 position in 1970-71, retained the position in 1971-72 when he pushed the record up to 71 points, and then came that season of seasons in 1975-76.

The one-time Kilkenny sharpshooter is also the only player to head the table nationally in either code over four separate programmes.

It is somewhat unusual, to say the least, that no hurler has come even close to Keher's peak, other than a forward from Kerry, a county that we do not generally associate with a challenging role in the race for the All-Ireland senior title.

Full marks, then, to John Hennessy in earning such a proud ranking in the review, a mere two points short of the Keher record milestone, and at a better match average than the one achieved by the Kilkenny artist in his big year.

Hennessy chalked up 12-54 (90 points) in eight games, at an average of 11.25 points a game, as compared with Keher's average of 8.36 points.

The Kerry man scored on every appearance, and he also took his place in the big-hitting stakes in the League as far as top individual returns are concerned, with a superb 3-10 against May at Aughamore in November 1990. Naturally enough, that was his best return for a single game in the series.

Hennessy's goals return in 1989-90 is not the best by a chart-leader for an annual programme. Christy Heffernan holds this distinction as a result of finishing ahead of the field in 1981-82 with a modest 46 points over-all. The one-time Kilkenny forward scored 13-7 in eight games, at an average of 5.75 points a match.

Ulster's only representative in the table is Des Donnelly (Antrim), who shared the leading spot in 1985-86 with David Kilcoyne (Westmeath).

The Glensman rattled home 9-41 (68 points) in seven ties at an impressive match average of 9.71 points. His total is understandably the record for a Northern hurler.

Jimmy Doyle (Tipperary), Francis Loughnane (Tipperary), Ned Buggy (Wexford) and Cyril Lyons (Clare) are the only hurlers, other than Keher, to head the annual review more than once.

Doyle was leading scorer in 1964-65, 1965-66 and 1967-68. Loughnane entered the exclusive list in 1972-73 with a then new record at 7-55 (76 points) in nine games, returned in 1974-75 and again in 1978-79. Buggy was top scorer in 1977-78 and 1980-81.

Lyons outscored all others in 1984-85 and 1986-87.

LEADING ANNUAL RETURNS

The leading annual returns for the National Leagues in hurling and football for a full season are:

HURLING

POINTS	PLAYER	SCORE	GAMES	AVERAGE	SEASON
92	E. Keher (Kilkenny)	11-59	11	8.36	1975-76
90	J. Hennessy (Kerry)	12-54	8	11.25	1989-90
76	F. Loughnane (Tipperary)	7-55	9	8.44	1972-73
72	P. Kelly (Limerick)	3-63	9	8.00	1982-83
72	J. Holohan (Wexford)	6-54	10	7.20	1990-91
71	E. Keher (Kilkenny)	5-56	9	7.88	1971-72
70	J. Dooley (Offaly)	1-67	8	8.75	1994-95
69	J. Grogan (Tipperary)	10-39	7	9.85	1983-84
68	D. Donnelly (Antrim)	9-41	7	9.71	1985-86
68	D. Kilcoyne (Westmeath)	3-59	8	8.50	1985-86

FOOTBALL

POINTS	PLAYER	SCORE	GAMES	AVERAGE	SEASON
79	G. Heavin (Westmeath)	7-58	11	7.18	1993-94
66	A. McTague (Offaly	0-66	9	7.33	1971-72
65	B. Stafford (Meath)	7.44	12	5.41	1989-90
64	M. Kcarins (Sligo)	0 64	9	7.11	1973-74
59	T. McTague (Offaly)	1-56	9	6.55	1972-73
58	B. Stafford (Meath)	2-52	11	5.27	1987-88
56	C. Daye (Wicklow)	5-41	8	7.00	1994-95
55	M. Connor (Offaly)	3-46	11	5.00	1981-82
54	M. Kearins (Sligo)	2-48	8	6.75	1970-71

TOP OF THE INDIVIDUAL CHARTS

The top scores on the individual charts for games in the National Leagues since 1955 are:

HURLING

22 points: Christy Ring (Cork) 6-4 v. Wexford at Cork in 1959.
19 points: Christy Heffernan (Kilkenny) 5-4 v. Carlow at Kilkenny in 1982.
Richie Melia (Meath) 5-4 v. Louth at Navan in 1971.
Brian Gilmore (Down) 6-1 v. Meath at Trim in 1980.
John Hennessy (Kerry) 3-10 v. Mayo at Aughamore in 1990.
18 points: Denis Heaslip (Kilkenny) 6-0 v. Offaly at Birr in 1962.
Des Donnelly (Antrim) 3-9 v. Meath at Glenravel in 1985.
17 points: Eddie Keher (Kilkenny) 2-11 v. Laois at Kilkenny in 1966.
Des Donnelly (Antrim) 3-8 v. Kerry at Tralee in 1986.
Nicholas English (Tipperary) 2-11 v. Waterford at Croke Park in 1988.
16 points: Eddie Keher (Kilkenny) 2-10 v. Offaly at Kilkenny in 1967.
Liam Dooley (Tipperary) 5-1 v. Kerry at Clonmel in 1958.
John McKenna (Tipperary) 5-1 v. Offaly at Birr in 1961.
Gerard Coulter (Down) 5-1 v. Monaghan at Aughamullen in 1983.
Paddy Christie (Meath) 4-4 v. Roscommon at Trim in March 1964.

FOOTBALL

23 points: Frankie Donnelly (Tyrone) 4-11 v. Fermanagh at Pomeroy in 1956.
20 points: Pat Hallissey (Tipperary) 5-5 v. Kilkenny at Callan in 1989.
19 points: James McCartan (Down) 5-4 v. Antrim at Newcastle in 1958.
18 points: Eamonn Goulding (Cork) 6-0 v. Carlow at Cork in 1957.
17 points: Mick O'Dwyer (Kerry) 2-11 v. Tipperary at Killarney in 1969.
16 points: Noel Normoyle (Clare) 3-7 v. Kilkenny at Ennis in 1986.
15 points: Sean O'Connell (Derry) 4-3 v. Armagh at Dungannon in 1967.
Michael Turley (Laois) 3-6 v. Monaghan at Scotstown in 1991.
Frannie Kelly (Tipperary) 4-3 v. Kilkenny at Ardfinnan in 1991.

Christy Ring ... Leading Scorer

FINALS HOT SHOTS

The leading individual returns in the National Hurling and Football League finals from 1960 up to and including 1995 are:

HURLING

POINTS **SCORE**

POINTS	SCORE	
13	3-4	Christy Ring (Cork) v. Tipperary at Croke Park in 1960.
12	0-12	Paddy Kelly (Limerick) v. Wexford at Thurles in 1984.
	2-6	Joe Cooney (Galway) v. Clare at Thurles in 1987.
11	2-5	Charlie McCarthy (Cork) v. New York, first leg, in New York in 1970.
	3-2	Tony Doran (Wexford) v. Limerick at Croke Park in 1973.
10	1-7	Jimmy Doyle (Tipperary) v. New York, second leg, in New York in 1964.
	1-7	Jimmy Doyle (Tipperary) v. New York, second leg, in New York in 1968.
	1-7	Eddie Keher (Kilkenny) v. Clare, replay, at Thurles in 1976.
	1-7	Joe Cooney (Galway) v. Tipperary at Croke Park in 1989.
	0-10	D.J. Carey (Kilkenny) v. New York in New York in 1990.
9	0-9	Jimmy Doyle (Tipperary) v. Cork at Croke Park in 1960.
	2-3	Phil Grimes (Waterford) v. New York, draw, at Croke Park in 1963.
	2-3	Jimmy Doyle (Tipperary) v. New York, first leg, in New York in 1965.
	2-3	Jack Ryan (Tipperary) v. Limerick at Cork in 1971.
	1-6	Ritchie Bennis (Limerick) v. Cork at Thurles in 1972.
	1-6	Tom Byrne (Wexford) v. Limerick at Croke Park in 1973.
	3-0	Eamonn O'Donoghue (Cork) v. Limerick at Limerick in 1974.
	3-0	Paddy Delaney (Kilkenny) v. Clare, replay, at Thurles in 1976.

1-6	Barry Egan (Cork) v. Wexford, second replay, at Thurles in 1993.
0-9	Jim Kehoe (Tipperary) v. Galway at Limerick in 1979.

FOOTBALL

POINTS	SCORE	
12	0-12	Tony McTague (Offaly) v. Kerry at Croke Park in 1973.
9	0-9	Mick O'Connell (Kerry) v. New York, second leg, in New York in 1969 after extra time.
	2-3	Brendan Lynch (Kerry) v. Offaly at Croke Park in 1973.
	1-6	Billy Fitzpatrick (Mayo) v. Dublin at Croke Park in 1978.
	0-8	Ollie O'Brien (Meath) v. Dublin at Croke Park in 1975.
	1-5	Michael Sheehy (Kerry) v. Galway at Limerick in 1984.
	1-5	Anthony Tohill (Derry) v. Tyrone at Croke Park in 1992

NATIONAL LEAGUES – TITLES WINNERS CHARTS

HURLING

16	Tipperary	1928,	1949,	1950,	1952,	1954,	1955,
		1957,	1959,	1960,	1961,	1964,	
		1965,	1968,	1979,	1988,	1994.	
13	Cork	1926,	1930,	1940,	1941,	1948,	1953,
		1969,	1970,	1972,	1974,	1980,	
		1981,	1993.				
10	Limerick	1934,	1935,	1936,	1937,	1938,	1947,
		1971,	1984,	1985,	1992.		
9	Kilkenny	1933,	1962,	1966,	1976,	1982,	1983,
		1986,	1990,	1995.			
5	Galway	1932,	1951,	1975,	1987,	1989.	

4	Wexford	1956,	1958,	1967,	1973.		
3	Clare	1946,	1977,	1978.			
2	Dublin	1929,	1939.				
1	Offaly	1991.					
1	Waterford	1963.					

FOOTBALL

15	Kerry	1928,	1929,	1931,	1932,	1959,	1961,
		1963,	1969,	1971,	1972,	1973,
		1974,	1977,	1982,	1984.	
10	Mayo	1934,	1935,	1936,	1937,	1938,	1939,
		1941,	1949,	1954,	1970.	
8	Dublin	1953,	1955,	1958,	1976,	1978,	1987,
		1991,	1993.	
7	Meath	1933,	1946,	1951,	1975,	1988,	1990,
		1994.	
4	Cork	1952,	1956,	1980,	1989.	
	Down	1960,	1962,	1968,	1983.	
	Galway	1940,	1957,	1965,	1981.	
3	New York	1950,	1964,	1967.	
	Derry	1947,	1992,	1995.	
2	Laois	1927,	1986.	
1	Cavan	1948.	
	Longford	1966.	
	Monaghan	1985.	
	Roscommon	1979.	

The National Leagues were suspended from 1942 to 1945 inclusive, due to World War II.

CAMOGIE

GOLDEN ERA OF THE DOWNEY TWINS

Seldom, if ever, have sisters dominated any ladies sport to the same remarkable extent as the Downey twins, Angela and Ann, of Kilkenny, in camogie. Their brilliance and above all dedication not only have kept them on top for a long, long spell, but contributed in the richest possible measure to a golden era for the Marble County in the All-Ireland senior championship.

Angela and Ann were both in the Kilkenny squad that made an historic break-through in 1974 by capturing the county's first All-Ireland senior title. Angela played in the final win over Cork in a replay, as well as in the drawn game. Ann was a substitute for those games, but did not make an appearance.

Who could have envisaged then that twenty-one years later they would still be turning on the style in an All-Ireland senior final winning show by Kilkenny?

The Downey sisters helped the

The Downey Twins ...
Angela and Ann

Noresiders to All-Ireland title wins in 1976, 1977 and 1981. Then in 1985, the county started off on a glorious reign that brought seven national crowns in succession up to and including 1991.

Angela, with her powerful play and, above all, expert finishing skills, and Ann at midfield, proved mighty influences in keeping Kilkenny on top in the championship for so long.

Angela can now point to appearances in every one of the county's twelve All-Ireland senior championship winning teams. She also captained Kilkenny in their successes of 1977, 1988 and 1991. Ann played in eleven deciders, was on the official substitutes' panel in 1974 and captained Kilkenny in 1989 and 1994.

In addition, the sisters have won All-Ireland club medals with St Paul's, National League souvenirs with the county senior team, and interprovincial awards with Leinster.

Their twelve All-Ireland senior medals have Angela and Ann in third place in the all-time rankings of All-Ireland medal winners, three short of pace-setting Kathleen Mills.

The Downey sisters are daughters of former All-Ireland senior hurler, Shem Downey. Both were in the team that lost the 1995 All-Ireland Senior Final to Cork and Angela announced her retirement after that game.

THE MILLS RECORD

Kathleen Mills was one of the all-time greats of the sport. She sparkled at a time when Dublin were rich in oustanding personalities.

Mills was an outstanding forward. She won her first All-Ireland senior medal in 1942 and helped Dublin to retain the title in 1943 and again the following season.

Antrim broke the Dubs run in 1945 and went on to make it three titles on the trot in 1947. Dublin returned to the top in 1948 and remained there without a break until 1955. Kathleen played in each of those title winning teams, except 1949.

There was an unusual Antrim-Cork final in 1956, but Dublin, with Mills again to the fore, regained the crown in 1957. A year later, she joined an exclusive company by captaining the Dubs to the O'Duffy Cup for the only time and collected medals again in 1959, 1960 and 1961.

The dynamic Dubliner then won her record total of 15 medals over a span that embraced three decades. Truly a player apart was Kathleen Mills!

ARMAGH DO IT AGAIN

Armagh completed a remarkable double after thirteen years when they beat Dublin at St Vincent's Ground, Marino, Dublin, by 3-8 to 2-1 in June 1993 in the National Junior League final. The Orchard County won the inaugural League final in this grade in 1980 and their 1993 success was recorded in the first 15-a-side final.

Ursula McGivern led Armagh from centre half forward to the 1993 title, and Joan Rice was their ace scoregetter, with 2-1.

Camogie teams have traditionally been composed of 12 players and it was back to the traditional format for the 1993 All-Ireland junior championship. Armagh qualified for the All-Ireland junior final against Galway at headquarters in September. A last minute goal by Carmel Hannon earned the Connacht champions a dramatic draw.

The replay drew a bumper attendance to Breffni Park in Cavan. The excellence of Margaret McKee in goal, Celine McGeary in the half back line and the accuracy of Patricia McEvoy, top scorer with 1-2, captain McGivern and Bernie McBride did much to blue-print a 2-10 to 0-6 win for Armagh.

The triumph gave the Northern county a first All-Ireland title and Ursula

McGivern took her place in the record-makers by leading the county to the big double. She had the double distinction of leading Armagh to a first junior championship and also of captaining the county to national titles in the same year with teams of 15-a-side and 12-a-side. A rare double in more ways than one.

LONG WAIT ENDS FOR QUEEN'S

The Universities' senior camogie championship was launched in 1915, but Queen's, Belfast, had to wait until 1991 for their first win. The long wait ended in exciting style on a February afternoon at Turloughmore, Co. Galway, where Queen's beat UCG by 3-6 to 1-3 in the final.

That record-making team had many stars. Róisín O'Neill, Deirdre Canning, in defence, Joan Tobin at midfield, and Brona McCann, Orla Higgins and Deirdre O'Doherty in attack were particularly impressive.

UNA O'CONNOR IN A SPECIAL CLASS

Una O'Connor ... remarkable record with Dublin

Una O'Connor not only established herself as a full forward supreme in the match-winning arts of making and taking of scores, but she also set a number of highly impressive records.

She regularly achieved impressive match returns in games at all levels, and in her own sport was on a par with the truly great scoring giants of football and hurling.

Dublin won ten All-Ireland senior championships in succession from 1957 to 1966, and Una O'Connor played in every winning side. That is a record for the sport, and brought the brilliant Dubliner's total of All-Ireland medals to thirteen.

In 1964, O'Connor won an All-Ireland inter-club medal with Celtic in the Jubilee championship. Having captained the Dubs in 1963 and 1964, she became the first player to win national medals at club, inter-county and interprovincial level, and also to captain an All-Ireland inter-county title winning combination.

Down's Winning Start

Moira Caldwell led Down as the Mourne county beat Cork in 1968 in the inaugural All-Ireland junior final. She played at midfield and made a big contribution to the win that gave Down custody of the New Ireland Cup.

Six years later, Down kept up the winning sequence. A gifted side, captained by Susan Lively from midfield, beat Cork 3-0 to 0-1 in the first All-Ireland minor final and were rewarded with the new Corn Tailteann.

Gradam Tailte

In 1982, the Camogie Association launched Gradam Tailte, which could be

described as the sport's own superstars competition. This featured the camogie player of the year in each county in a competition over a number of disciplines or exercises, covering athletics, basketball, gym and camogie skills.

Josephine McClements, of Antrim, was the first winner.

Pictured alongside is Clare Cronin, Cork ... second Gradam Tailte winner receiving the award from Mary Fennelly, then President of the Camogie Association

Only Scorer

Camogie provides one of the most interesting and unusual scoring achievements I have on record. In a 1959 Dublin League game, Patsy Rowan, of Civil Service, scored 7-1 (22 points) against Austin Stacks.

Apart from the fact that the total was a highly impressive one in its own right, Patsy Rowan also gained the almost unbelievable distinction of being the only player to score in that match! Austin Stacks failed to raise a solitary flag, and Rowan was her club's only scorer.

First For Riordan

Cally Riordan, from Youghal, blazed an unique trail in 1973 when she played in the All-Ireland junior and senior finals on the same afternoon. She was the first to achieve such a proud distinction.

Riordan was full forward in the junior side in their win over Galway and scored 1-1 as well. Then in the senior final she went in as a substitute against Antrim and collected a second national medal. Both games were at Croke Park.

Club Double

Ann Carroll, who was born in London, won an All-Ireland senior club medal with St Patrick's, Glengoole-Ballingarry, Tipperary, in 1965. A year later, she was top scorer in the final as St Patrick's maintained their grip on the title by beating St Paul's, Kilkenny, in the final.

In 1968, Ann played in her third club final, but in the colours of St Paul's, Kilkenny. She was also top scorer with 4-1 as the Noresiders beat Ahane, of Limerick, and Carroll became the first player to win All-Ireland club medals with different teams – and also from different provinces!

What A Year For Lynn!

Lynn Dunlea dominated the 1993 camogie season in big way and over a variety of competitions. She helped Cork to win the Munster junior championship and was sent in as a substitute in the All-Ireland senior semi-final against Kilkenny at Nowlan Park in August.

It proved an inspired substitution for Cork as, thirty seconds from time, Dunlea crashed home a dramatic goal to earn her side a sensational and last gasp one point win.

She was Cork's top scorer with 2-1 in the All-Ireland final win over Galway. At the end of the year Dunlea stamped her personality in a big way on the All-Ireland club final win with Glen Rovers by scoring a thundering 4-5 against Mullagh, Galway. All that at only 20 years of age!

Captain – Junior And Senior

Nancy O'Driscoll captained Cork to their first All-Ireland junior title in 1973. Five years later she led the Leesiders from midfield to victory in the All-Ireland senior final to become the first to lead a county to national success in both grades.

O`Driscoll gained another distinction in that match. The Cork captain and left midfielder, as well as full forward Mary Geaney, became the first hockey internationals to win All-Ireland senior camogie medals.

In the junior final, played on the same day in 1978 as the curtain-raiser to the senior summit, Caroline McWilliams was prominent at midfield for Derry in their All-Ireland victory over Cork. She made a quick journey from Edinburgh, where she was engaged in hockey internationals the day before the camogie decider and so became the first hockey international to win a camogie All-Ireland medal in any grade.

THE ALL-IRELAND RANKINGS

This is how the counties measure up in the All-Ireland championships:

SENIOR

26	Dublin	1932,	1933,	1937,	1938,	1942,	1943,
		1944,	1948,	1949,	1950,	1951,	1952,
		1953,	1954,	1955,	1957,	1958,	1959,
		1960,	1961,	1962,	1963,	1964,	1965,
		1966,	1984.				
17	Cork	1934,	1935,	1936,	1939,	1940,	1941,
		1970,	1971,	1972,	1973,	1978,	1980,
		1982,	1983,	1992,	1993,	1995.	
12	Kilkenny	1974,	1976,	1977,	1981,	1985,	1986,
		1987,	1988,	1989,	1990,	1991,	1994.
6	Antrim	1945,	1946,	1947,	1956,	1967,	1979.
3	Wexford	1968,	1969,	1975.			

JUNIOR

5	Galway	1972,	1979,	1985,	1988,	1994.
4	Cork	1973,	1980,	1983,	1984.	
3	Dublin	1970,	1971,	1975.		
3	Clare	1974,	1981,	1986.		
	Down	1968,	1976,	1991.		
	Dublin	1970,	1971,	1975.		
	Kildare	1987,	1989,	1990.		
2	Derry	1969,	1978.			
2	Limerick	1977,	1995			
2	Tipperary	1981,	1992.			
1	Armagh	1993.				
	Louth	1982.				

MINOR

8	Cork	1975,	1976,	1978,	1979,	1980,	1983,
		1984	1985.				
5	Galway	1977,	1981,	1986,	1987,	1994.	
3	Kilkenny	1988,	1989,	1991.			
	Tipperary	1990,	1992,	1993.			
1	Down	1974.					
	Dublin	1982.					
	Wexford	1995					

INTERMEDIATE

2	Clare	1993	1995
1	Dublin	1992	
	Armagh	1994	

*Cally Riordan, who achieved a unique medals double in 1973
(see page 41), is second from left in the back row in the Cork side
that won the 1970 All-Ireland senior title.*

GAMES ABROAD

REMARKABLE PLACE FOR O'REILLY

The late John Joe O'Reilly, of Cavan, was a centre half back of the highest calibre, cool, efficient, always on his game and one of the best county captains ever in the history of football.

He led Ulster to their first Railway Cup football title in 1942 and was Cavan's captain in their finest hour – the 1947 All-Ireland final win over Kerry in sweltering heat at the Polo Grounds in New York.

That ranks as the only All-Ireland senior final in either code played outside of this country. O'Reilly left his stamp on the unique match in a really big way. Fifteen minutes into the game, the Northerners trailed by eight points.

However, the Ulster champions, prompted by their magnificent centre half back and captain, found their best form, so much so that they rallied so well that they led by 2-5 to 2-4 at the interval.

Cavan kept up the momentum in the second half. They turned on a particularly impressive showing to eventually win the most important final played by 2-11 to 2-7.

O'Reilly captained Cavan to their successful defence of the Sam Maguire Cup in 1948. He became the only man to captain All-Ireland title winning teams at senior level in two continents, and the first and only Ulster man so far to be twice presented with the Sam Maguire Cup.

John Joe O'Reilly was born in Kilmore, Killeshandra, and had a brilliant career from Colleges' ranks up to senior. He died unexpectedly in November 1952.

The 1947 final was noteworthy for a sharpshooting display by Peter Donoghue, whose exhibition had American sportswriters calling him the "Babe Ruth" of Gaelic football.

The Polo Grounds, now no more, was then a famed baseball pitch and Babe Ruth was a giant of that time in the sport and one of the all-time greats of baseball.

Donoghue, a superb free-taker, was in magical form in that game. He expertly rifled over eight of Cavan's eleven points to write his name in extra large letters in the story of the county's most famous victory.

Centre half forward for Cavan and one of their match-winners was Mick

Higgins, who was born in New York. He went on to win a second All-Ireland medal a year later and led the Breffni County to their last All-Ireland senior title win in 1952.

The New York final attracted an attendance of 34,941 and Mayor O'Dwyer threw in the ball.

The match was played on a rock hard surface in sweltering heat and Kerry opened in whirlwind fashion. Gega O'Connor, Kerry's full forward, opened the scoring with a point. Batt Garvey scored the first goal and Donoghue hit Cavan's first score, a point.

Midfielder Eddie Dowling scored Kerry's second goal. The Ulster champions rallied strongly after that and goals by Joe Stafford and Mick Higgins put them in the driver's seat.

Kerry were defending champions and were captained by their right full back Denny Lyne, who was also their No. 2 in the final win the year previous.

Dan O'Keeffe went into that game as Kerry's goalkeeper with a then record seven All-Ireland senior medals to his credit. The Polo Grounds game marked the final appearance of the net-minder in a Sam Maguire Cup tie.

O'Keeffe made a winning debut in an All-Ireland senior football final in 1931. His other glory years were 1932, 1937, 1939, 1940, 1941 and 1946. He played in ten finals in the All-Ireland senior football championship and three replays.

The game was refereed by Martin O'Neill (Wexford), who had charge of the 1932 final between Kerry and Mayo and the 1933 Cavan-Galway encounter.

The game was broadcast live by Radio Éireann, as the station was then known, and that was quite an achievement at the time.

Bill Doonan, left, and Paddy Kennedy (Kerry) race for possession near the Cavan goal in the historic 1947 Final in New York.

THE PRESIDENTS

OUT ON THEIR OWN – MACFLYNN AND BOOTHMAN

Pádraig MacFlynn and Jack Boothman command special places in the ranks of Presidents of the GAA.

MacFlynn became the 26th man elected to the post when chosen for the three year term starting in 1979. However, unlike those honoured before then, the Down official was elected to the position a year earlier.

Well, not exactly as President. Instead, MacFlynn became the first to be elected to the newly created post of President-Elect when chosen for that role at the Annual Congress at Ballina in 1978.

The Down official, a native of Magherafelt, Derry, became the fourth Ulster man to succeed to the post of President. The first, Patrick McNamee, of Antrim, made history on the double.

Apart from the fact that he brought Ulster into the review when chosen in 1938, he went on to remain in the post for five years. What was unusual about that at the time was that, by then, the term of office had been limited to three years. However, the Northerner proved so popular that his term was extended by two years.

Boothman, a former President of the Leinster Council, was elected President-Elect in 1993 in Dublin and took over the No. 1 position in administration of the organisation at the Annual Congress in Ballyconnell, Cavan, in 1994.

Boothman is the first member of the Church of Ireland to succeed to the position. Born in Kildare and now resident in Wicklow, he has given much of his life to the GAA. He has held executive positions with Blessington club.

Maurice Davin of Tipperary was the first GAA President and also the only man to hold the position over two separate or distinct terms, He was first chosen in 1884, resigned in 1887, and returned to office in 1888. He resigned again the following year.

Jim Nowlan of Kilkenny was the longest serving President. He was elected chairman when the Leinster Council was formed in 1900 and, after Michael Deering died in office in March 1901, the Noresider acted as President until that year's Congress at Thurles. Nowlan was then unanimously elected to the post and held the office without a break until the 1921 Congress in Dublin. Jim

47

Pádraig Mac Flynn, first President-Elect is presented with his Presidential Seal of Office by Con Murphy (Cork).

Nowlan is commemorated today by the magnificent Nowlan Park in Kilkenny City.

A Kilkenny man, Paddy Buggy, who won an All-Ireland senior medal in hurling in 1957, was President during the Centenary Year of 1984. His reign was from 1982 to 1985.

Connacht's first President of modern times was Leitrim-born Dan O'Rourke, who was associated with Roscommon, and was elected in 1946.

Pat Fanning of Waterford was President when the Annual Congress of 1971, held at Queen's University, Belfast, removed from the Official Guide the then 66-year-old Rule 27. That was the rule that prohibited members of the GAA from playing, attending or promoting rugby, soccer, hockey or cricket.

THE PRESIDENTS

The following is the complete list of Presidents of the Gaelic Athletic Association over the years:

1884	M Davin (Tipperary)	1949	M Kehoe (Wexford)
1887	EM Bennett (Clare)	1952	MV O'Donoghue (Waterford)
1888	M Davin (Tipperary)	1955	S McFerran (Antrim)
1899	PJ Kelly (Galway)	1958	JJ Stewart (Dublin)
1895	FB Dineen (Limerick)	1961	H Byrne (Wicklow)
1898	M Deering (Cork)	1964	A Murray (Armagh)
1901	J Nowlan (Kilkenny)	1967	S O'Riain (Tipperary)
1921	D McCarthy (Dublin)	1970	P Fanning (Waterford)
1924	PB Breen (Wexford)	1973	D Keenan (Roscommon)
1926	WP Clifford (Limerick)	1976	C Murphy (Cork)
1928	S Ryan (Dublin)	1979	P Mac Flynn (Down)
1932	S McCarthy (Cork)	1982	P Buggy (Kilkenny)
1935	R O'Keeffe (Laois)	1985	M Loftus (Mayo)
1938	P McNamee (Antrim)	1988	J Dowling (Offaly)
1943	S Gardiner (Tipperary)	1991	P Quinn (Fermanagh)
1946	D O'Rourke (Roscommon)	1994	J Boothman (Wicklow)

Pictured alongside is Jack Boothman ... history maker

49

All-Ireland "B" Football

Mickey Quinn Ushers In New Era

Mickey Quinn ushered in a new era in football when he led Leitrim from right midfield to their first national title by beating Sligo convincingly by 2-11 to 0-2 at Dr Hyde Park, Roscommon, on November 11, 1990. The win was recorded in the first All-Ireland "B" football championship final.

Ciarán Mahon was the ace marksman in that game with 1-4. The goal was scored from a penalty after fifteen minutes. The second goal of the championship came after some 21 minutes and was sent home by right half forward Pádraig Kenny.

The second final was played at Ballinasloe and Clare captured their first major trophy in 62 years by beating Longford by six points after extra time. The only goal came 15 seconds into the additional time and was scored by Clare's left full forward, David Keane.

The match was a double triumph for Gerry Killeen, Clare's left half forward. He proved to be a matchwinner with his sharp finishing, scoring 7 points, and also was a splendid captain for the Banner County.

The 1992 final was played on a wet

John Newton (Roscommon) about to be challenged by Leitrim's Padraig Kenny and Mickey Quinn as Shane Heslin (background) watches – Connacht Championship semi-final in Carrick-on-Shannon

and windy December afternoon at Navan, but the conditions did not dampen the enthusiasm of Wicklow footballers as Kevin O'Brien lifted the Cup in triumph after a hard-earned four points win over Antrim.

The success marked Wicklow's first All-Ireland title in the adult grade of football, although Bray Emmets won the national senior championship of 1902, but represented Dublin.

When mighty Wicklow midfielder Pat O'Byrne was unable to line out before the start, Darren Behan was called up from the substitutes bench in place of Seán O'Brien, who moved back from attack to fill the midfield vacancy created by the absence of O'Byrne. Behan celebrated by collecting the solitary goal after 22 minutes. Antrim scored just a single point against the wind in the first half. Seán O'Brien had an outstanding game at midfield, and Kevin O'Brien, with his cultured and intelligent football in attack, was another to play an important part in the unique triumph.

Behan headed the scoring ranks with his goal.

No Joy For Sligo – Yet Again

Sligo became the first county to make two appearances in an All-Ireland "B" football championship final when they met Laois at Pearse Park, Longford, on November 14, 1993. However, there was again no joy for the North-Connacht men in the first final that failed to produce a single goal.

Laois were the superior team and won comfortably by twelve points. The sharpshooting of left full forward Damien Delaney was a key factor in the O'Moore County success. He hit seven points, six from frees.

Midfielder Denis Lalor, with his clever football and leadership as captain, and Hugh Emerson and Leo Turley, both in attack, were other leading campaigners in the winning effort. Delaney, not surprisingly, led the scoring returns.

The championship, for teams beaten in the early stages of the provincial senior campaigns, has proved a worthwhile addition to the GAA calendar and gives the so-called weaker counties an added incentive each year.

Antrim are the only Ulster county to have appeared in a final to date.

The following are the results:

1990	Leitrim 2-11; Sligo 0-2, at Roscommon
1991	Clare 1-12; Longford 0-9, at Ballinsloe, after extra time
1992	Wicklow 1-5; Antrim 0-4, at Navan
1993	Laois 0-17; Sligo 0-5, at Longford
1994	Carlow 2-10; Westmeath 1-11, at Tullamore
1995	Tipperary 2-12; Longford 2-5, at Birr

All-Ireland "B" Hurling

Accurate Walshe Set Early Trend

The accuracy of Kildare right half forward Johnny Walshe illuminated the first All-Ireland "B" hurling championship final played at Croke Park on June 23, 1974. He was in sparkling form against Antrim, and was a big difference between the sides.

Walshe helped himself to 0-10 as Kildare became the initial winners of the title on a 1-26 to 3-13 score line. Willie Richmond of Antrim scored the first goal in a final twenty-two minutes into the game. He filled the No. 14 berth.

The final attracted only a few hundred spectators.

A year later, Westmeath beat Kerry at Limerick in the first "home" final and drew with London in the final proper. That game featured a sharpshooting performance by Westmeath's Mick Flanagan, who helped himself to a then new individual scoring standard for the series at 3-2.

That return recorded at headquarters is now only good enough to include Flanagan in a group of four hurlers on eleven points in a ranking at No. 3 in the top scoring individual chart. The goals feat by the Westmeath man is one of the top two peaks in this regard in a final. Mick Moore scored 3-1 for Kildare against London at Ruislip, London, in 1990. Phil Dillon did much to engineer a first final win by Laois when he helped himself to 0-13 against London at Croke Park in 1977 and this now leads the way in the chart of top scorers for the finals proper.

In the inaugural "B" championship in 1974, Hertfordshire represented Britain and lost in a semi-final replay at Luton to Antrim in a high scoring game by 5-15 to 4-13. Since then, London has appeared in every final and lead the Roll of Honour with four title wins.

Counties from all provinces have appeared in the concluding round. Kildare, Westmeath, Kerry, Laois and Roscommon all had winning final debuts.

Meath had their first outing in a summit in 1985 in what proved an historic game on two counts. The Royal County lost by two points at Trim to London, who made it a case of "lucky thirteen" by chalking up their first triumph in thirteen successive finals.

Meath did not return to the final action until 1993. They travelled to Ruislip, where the excellent finishing of Pat Potterton brightened the game. He slotted over eleven points in expert fashion to pave the way for a memorable win by

2-16 to 1-16.

Carlow lost their initial summit in 1987 to London and, like Meath, bounced back to celebrate a golden day in 1992 at Ruislip, where they beat the Exiles by 2-15 to 3-10.

Roscommon celebrated their Final debut in 1994 at Ruislip where a late Michael Cunniffe point ensured a 1-10 to 1-9 win over home side London.

The All-Ireland "B" champions earn a preliminary round tie or a quarter-final in the chase for the Liam McCarthy Cup each year. Antrim alone of the "B" winners have the distinction of having met opposition from the "B" series in an All-Ireland quarter-final.

After winning their last "B" crown in 1982, the Northern County has competed each year in the All-Ireland series proper (except in 1992, when Down won out in Ulster) and have met the "B" champions in six quarter-final ties. Antrim won them all.

ALL-IRELAND "B" HURLING CHAMPIONSHIP

ROLL OF HONOUR

5	London	1985,	1987,	1988,	1990,	1995.
3	Antrim	1978,	1981,	1982.		
	Kerry	1976,	1983,	1986.		
	Kildare	1974,	1980,	1989.		
	Westmeath	1975,	1984,	1991.		
2	Laois	1977,	1979.			
1	Carlow	1992.				
	Meath	1993.				
	Roscommon	1994.				

The leading individual scoring feats in "B" finals proper are:

POINTS SCORE

13	0-13	Phil Dillon (Laois) v. London at Croke Park, in 1977
12	1-9	Frank Keenan (Laois) v. London in replay at Athy, in 1979
	0-12	Johnny Walshe (Kildare) v. London at Croke Park, in 1980
11	3-2	Mick Flanagan (Westmeath) v. London at Ruislip, in 1984
	1-8	David Kilcoyne (Westmeath) v. London at Ruislip, in 1984
	1-8	Michael Connolly (London) v. Kildare at Ruislip, in 1990
	0-11	Pat Potterton (Meath) v. London at Ruislip, in 1993

TEXACO AWARDS

MCKEEVER AND WALL BLAZED THE TRAIL

Jim McKeever, Tony Wall, James McCartan, Kevin Heffernan and Jack O'Shea rank as the trail blazers in the Texaco annual award winners in football and hurling.

McKeever led Derry in majestic style to their All-Ireland senior football final debut in 1958. The Foylesiders lost that historic game to Dublin, but the Derry captain, a prince of midfielders, was later chosen as the first Caltex, now Texaco, award winner in 1958 in football.

McKeever was to rank as the only man to win a trophy in football without winning an All-Ireland senior medal the previous September until 1974. Then, ironically, Kevin Heffernan, who led Dublin to their 1958 win over Derry, was chosen in the code. Earlier that year, he managed the Dubs side that beat Galway to capture the Sam Maguire Cup for the first time in eleven years.

In the meantime, only one footballer has been honoured in any year without winning an All-Ireland senior medal the same season. Colm O'Rourke found favour in 1991, even though Meath lost the Sam Maguire Cup tie to Down.

O'Rourke only went into the final seven and a half minutes into the second half, due to an illness, and gave a new status and authority to the attack with his ability to win possession and initiate movements that spearheaded a dramatic revival.

Down were six points ahead when O'Rourke made his entry, and in the end won by just a brace of points. Meath played ten championship games that season and O'Rourke not only appeared in every one, but showed up really well in each match into the bargain.

James McCartan, a brilliant figure in the Down team that electrified the nation in the early 'Sixties, by bringing the Sam Maguire Cup across the Border for the first time, was the first man in either code to win two trophies.

McCartan's contribution to Down's win over Kerry in 1960 brought an added bonus with his selection as footballer of the year. A year later, he helped the Mourne County to retain the Cup and retained the faith of the Texaco selectors.

Tony Wall led Tipperary to victory over Galway in the All-Ireland senior hurling final of 1958 and later that year joined McKeever as the trail setter in the Texaco honours as hurler of the year.

The following season, the legendary Christy Ring was chosen, even though Cork did not win out in Munster that year.

Since then, the All-Ireland senior champions of each year have provided the Texaco award winner, except in 1976, when Tony Doran (Wexford) was the selection, and 1992, when Brian Corcoran (Cork) found favour.

Cork and Kilkenny were All-Ireland champions in those seasons.

Jimmy Keaveney became only the second player in either code to be twice honoured. He was chosen for the first time in 1976 and the Dubliner retained his spot the following season.

Jack O'Shea joined the exclusive ranks in 1980 and 1981. Three seasons later, the great Kerry midfielder was back for a third award and in 1985 he collected a fourth. As a result, he is the most honoured player in the annals of this prestigious promotion.

Surprisingly enough, no hurler has been selected more than once.

Tony O'Sullivan and Shea Fahy helped to forge out a special place for Cork when chosen in hurling and football respectively in 1990. That was the first (and, so far, only) time that a single county provided both winners in the same season. Cork, of course, won the Liam McCarthy Cup and the Sam Maguire Cup that year.

Ollie Walsh (Kilkenny) 1967, Noel Skehan (Kilkenny) 1982 and Ger Cunningham (Cork) 1986, hurling, and Billy Morgan (Cork) 1973 and Martin Furlong (Offaly) 1982, football, rank as the only goalkeepers honoured.

The leading award winners, all in football, are:

4	Jack O'Shea (Kerry)	1980,	1981,	1984,	1985
2	Jimmy Keaveney (Dublin)	1976,	1977		
	James McCartan (Down)	1960,	1961		
	Pat Spillane (Kerry)	1978,	1986		

No hurler has been honoured more than once.

Jack O'Shea

55

ALL-IRELAND COLLEGES' CHAMPIONSHIPS

WINSTON QUICKLY ON GOALS STANDARD

Kevin Winston of Letterkenny scored what must rank as one of the quickest goals in an All-Ireland Colleges' senior football final. He lined out at left full forward for St Jarlath's, Tuam, against favourites St Patrick's, Maghera, in the 1994 final at Longford.

A mere thirty seconds after the throw-in, Winston had the ball in the Derry net, and Jarlath's went on to record a convincing 3-11 to 0-9 win.

Kevin is maintaining a proud family tradition in the game. He is son of Joe, a former Donegal county forward and sharpshooter. Joe won Ulster senior medals in 1972 and 1974 and was ace marksman for the 1972 Ulster senior championship, with 0-26 in four games, or 6.50 points a game on average.

It was a case of "fourth final lucky" for Jarlath's, the specialists of the All-Ireland senior championship, in the 'Nineties. They lost the summits of 1990, 1992 and 1993, but really made amends with a power-packed display in the '94 encounter with St Patrick's.

That win brought St Jarlath's record to eleven All-Ireland senior football championships since the second final in 1947.

Jarlath's were also involved in the first All-Ireland summit a year earlier. They met St Patrick's, Armagh, at Croke Park in May 1946 and were beaten by the brilliance of Iggy Jones.

One player never wins any game on his own, but Jones certainly played more than one man's part in bringing the title to Armagh. He stole the show in exciting fashion with a majestic performance and scored 3-4 – a tally that still commands top spot in the list of major individual scoring feats in Colleges' football finals. He went on to star as a senior with Tyrone.

Jarlath's and St Patrick's, Armagh, met in the second final and that game, too, saw one player stamp his personality on the exchanges in a big way. Sean Purcell, who, like Jones, went on to capture plenty of headlines as a senior with Galway, lined out at midfield for the Westerners.

He had an outstanding game as he roamed all over the field, helping out in defence, working tirelessly in the centre and prompting the attack in great style. Purcell also contributed six points to the Jarlath's return of 4-10.

Jarlath's also helped to write history in another area. They met Coláiste Chríost

Rí at Croke Park, in 1983, in what was the first Colleges' final televised live by RTE.

Coláiste Chríost Rí, Cork, had double cause for celebration in 1968. They made their debut in an All-Ireland football final and beat Belcamp OMI, Dublin, to become the first Munster side to capture the Hogan Cup.

Left midfielder Der Cogan skippered the Cork team and left half forward Billy Cogan was on the target with 1-5.

Kerry got in on the act a year later. John O'Keeffe, who went on to capture many headlines with Kerry as a senior, led St Brendan's, Killarney, from centre half back to victory over St Mary's, Galway.

FOUR IN A ROW

The hurling championship, unlike football, commenced in 1944 and opened with a great run by St Flannan's, Ennis. They beat St Kieran's, Kilkenny, at Thurles in April 1944 in the decider and the trophy was presented to the winning captain, J Minogue, by the then president of the GAA, Séamus Gardiner (Tipperary).

Flannan's were trained by famed Clare hurler Tull Considine.

Flannan's went on to make it four All-Ireland titles in a row in 1947, and Jimmy Smyth played in the 1945 to 1947 teams. He later became one of Clare's best ever hurlers and an outstanding sharpshooter.

The championships were suspended after the 1948 tests and were not revived until 1957.

Two years later, St Joseph's, Fairview, captained by Des Foley, brought the Hogan Cup to Dublin for the first time. Foley led Dublin in 1958 to the All-Ireland minor football title, and was the Metropolitan's captain when they captured the Sam Maguire Cup in 1963.

St Kieran's took over as the title specialists in hurling in 1993 by beating Our Lady's, Gort, for a twelfth crown. They have one more than the long-time pace-setters, St Flannan's.

St Mary's, Galway, failed in 1994 in the latest bid by a Western side to bring hurling's trophy, the Croke Cup, to Connacht for the first time.

The Galway boys beat St Kieran's in a semi-final after extra time and were well fancied to outscore North Monastery, Cork, in the summit at Nenagh. A goal from a penalty about ten minutes from the end by centre half back Kevin Egan, brother of senior sharpshooter, Barry, cliniched a 1-10 to 1-6 win for the "Mon" and their first title in nine years.

Interprovincial championships provided the main interest nationally for students and supporters of the national games from 1927 to the start of the All-Ireland individual series.

The interprovincial tests were revived when the All-Ireland individual tests were suspended from 1948 until 1957 and have not been played since.

St Jarlath's, Tuam ... winners of the Centenary Year All-Ireland Colleges Senior Football Title

ALL-IRELAND ROLL CALL
FOOTBALL

11	St Jarlath's, Tuam	1947,	1958,	1960,	1961,
		1964,	1966,	1974,	1978,
		1982,	1984,	1994.	
5	St Colman's, Newry	1967,	1975,	1986,	1988,
		1993.			
4	Coláiste Chríost Rí, Cork	1968,	1970,	1983,	1985.
	St Mel's, Longford	1948,	1962,	1963,	1987.
3	Carmelite College, Moate	1976,	1980,	1981.	
	St Patrick's, Maghera	1989,	1990,	1995.	
2	St Brendan's, Killarney	1969,	1992.		
1	Árd Scoil Rís, Dublin	1979.			
	Franciscan College, Gormanston	1973.			
	St Columb's, Derry	1965.			
	St Colman's, Claremorris	1977.			
	St Fachtna's, Skibbereen	1991.			
	St Joseph's, Fairview, Dublin	1959.			
	St Mary's, Belfast	1971.			
	St Nathy's, Ballaghaderreen	1957.			
	St Patrick's, Armagh	1946.			
	St Patrick's, Cavan	1972.			

HURLING

12	St Kieran's, Kilkenny	1948,	1957,	1959,	1961,
		1965,	1971,	1975,	1988,
		1989,	1990,	1992,	1993.
11	St Flannan's, Ennis	1944,	1945,	1946,	1947,
		1958,	1976,	1979,	1982,
		1983,	1987,	1991.	
5	St Finbarr's, Farranferris, Cork	1963,	1969,	1972,	1974,
		1984.			
	North Monastery, Cork	1960,	1970,	1980,	1985,
		1994.			
4	St Peter's, Wexford	1962,	1967,	1968,	1973.
2	Limerick CBS	1964,	1966.		
1	Kilkenny CBS	1981.			
	St Brendan's Comm. School, Birr	1986.			
	St Colman's, Fermoy	1977.			
	St Raphaels, Loughrea	1995			
	Templemore CBS	1978.			

Showing The Final Way

The following are the top individual scoring returns in All-Ireland Colleges' senior championships finals:

Hurling

Points Score

14	4-2	B. McMahon (St Flannan's, Ennis) v. Mount St Joseph's, Roscrea, 1947.
	4-2	Frank O'Brien, (St. Finbarr's, Farranferris) v. St. Kieran's, Kilkenny, at Thurles, 1969.
	2-8	Tony O'Sullivan (North Monastery, Cork) v. Birr Community School, at Thurles, 1980.
12	4-0	Joe Ryan (St Kieran's, Kilkenny) v. St Finbarr's, Farranferris, at Thurles, 1971.
	2-6	Richard Grace (Limerick CBS) v. St Peter's, Wexford, draw at Portlaoise, 1967.
	3-3	DJ Carey (St Kieran's, Kilkenny) v. St Flannan's, Ennis, at Nenagh, 1989.

Football

Points Score

13	3-4	Iggy Jones (St Patrick's, Armagh) v. St Jarlath's, Tuam, at Croke Park, 1946.
11	3-2	O. Reilly (St Patrick's, Cavan) v. St Mel's, Longford, 1948.
10	2-4	Billy Field (Coláiste Chríost Rí, Cork) v. St Malachy's, Belfast, at Croke Park, 1970.
8	1-5	Billy Cogan (Coláiste Chríost Rí, Cork) v. Belcamp OMI, Dublin, at Croke Park, 1968.
	1-5	Ciarán O'Keeffe (St Patrick's, Cavan) v. St Brendan's, Killarney, at Croke Park, 1972.
	1-5	Oliver Reel (St Colman's, Newry) v. St David's, Artane, Dublin, at Portlaoise, 1986.

Universities' Championships

Sigerson Cup
Paddy O'Hara Shaped
Northern History

Paddy O'Hara, the one-time Antrim inter-county senior footballer, commands a prominent place in the annals of Queen's, Belfast, in the Sigerson Cup, the Universities' senior football championship.

O'Hara played with Queen's in 1944-45 and was in the Antrim team that lost an All-Ireland senior semi-final to Kerry in 1946. In the early 'Fifties, he took over at Queen's as team trainer and manager and guided the University to their first Sigerson Cup final win in the 1958 series.

That long hoped for breakthrough came in February 1959 at Ballybay in a final replay against UCD. The Belfast students rallied from arrears of five points at the break to win by 0-10 to 0-9.

O'Hara was still there as team trainer-manager when Queen's regained the Cup in 1964 with another win over UCD. Seán O'Neill was the hero of that final win at Casement Park. He gave a superb display at full forward, and also finished top scorer on the day with 2-2.

O'Hara withdrew from his post with Queen's in 1970 because of business commitments and is best known these days as a commentator on Gaelic Games on both BBC and RTE.

Seán O'Neill was a member of the side that brought the Cup in triumph to Ulster for the first time in the 1958 final, as well as that 1964 team. Incidentally, Queen's were captained to their historic win of 1958 by left midfielder Hugh O'Kane (Antrim).

When Queen's won the Cup for the fourth time in 1982, Seán O'Neill was back in a big way. The Down man was team manager.

The Queen's success of 1958 broke the Dublin, Cork and Galway dominance of the title that had held sway since the inaugural championship of 1911.

Cork won the first championship, and Galway were winners a year later. Dublin, who were to go on and dominate the series, did not win their first title until 1915, but went on to record four championships in a row.

Dublin University made their debut in 1963, but have still to win the Cup.

The 'Seventies saw the competition widened further. Firstly, St Patrick's, Maynooth, took their place in the line-up in 1972, and had not long to wait for a first title win. That came at Croke Park in 1976, following a final win over UCD. Eamonn Whelan (Laois) and Paddy Henry (Sligo) at midfield, Tony O'Keeffe (Kerry) and Dan O'Mahoney (Mayo) in defence and Peter Burke (Longford) and Martin Nugent (Offaly) were stars of the 2-5 to 0-9 win.

The New University of Ulster at Coleraine entered the scene in 1976, and later came the University of Jordanstown and St Mary's, Belfast.

Gerard Houlahan (Armagh) and Enda Gormley (Derry), who were team mates in the 1993 All Stars selection, shared the scoring spotlight as they starred for Jordanstown when the University captured the Sigerson Cup for the first time with a 1-8 to 1-5 win over UCC at the Mardyke, Cork, in 1986. Houlahan hit 1-2 and Gormley, who had an outstanding match, scored five points.

Jordanstown went on to become the first Ulster side to retain the title by beating UCC again in the final by 0-6 to 0-4 at Bellaghy. Gormley was top scorer for the winners, with three points.

St Mary's, Belfast, became the third winners from Ulster in 1989. John Rehill (Fermanagh) led the Belfast students in brilliant fashion from midfield to a 3-13 to 1-5 win over defending champions UCC in Dublin.

This was St Mary's final debut and came in only their second season in the Sigerson Cup. The first half was a low scoring affair, with each side scoring just three points. However, the Northern attack really went on the rampage in the second half. Martin Houlihan, with a goal, and full forward Fergal McCann, with two goals, set the scene for the runaway win.

Dr George Sigerson of Strabane presented the trophy for the Universities championship. He was then a professor at UCD.

THE WINNING YEARS

32	University College, Dublin	1915,	1916,	1917,	1918,
		1920,	1923,	1926,	1928,
		1929,	1930,	1931,	1932,
		1935,	1944,	1945,	1946,
		1947,	1949,	1953,	1955,
		1956,	1957,	1959,	1961,
		1968,	1973,	1974,	1975,
		1977,	1978,	1979,	1985.
22	University College, Galway	1912,	1921,	1933,	1934,
		1936,	1937,	1938,	1939,
		1940,	1941,	1942,	1948,
		1950,	1954,	1960,	1962,

		1963,	1980,	1981,	1983,
		1984,	1992.		
19	University College, Cork	1911,	1913,	1914,	1919,
		1922,	1924,	1925,	1927,
		1943,	1951,	1952,	1965,
		1966,	1969,	1970,	1972,
		1988,	1994,	1995.	
6	Queen's University, Belfast	1958,	1964,	1971,	1982,
		1990,	1993.		
3	University of Ulster, Jordanstown	1986,	1987,	1991.	
1	St Mary's, Belfast	1989.			
1	St Patrick's, Maynooth	1976.			

Note: No Sigerson Cup Competition was held in 1967. After the 1966 series, the timing of the Sigerson Cup was changed from the autumn to the spring and 1967 was a blank season

FITZGIBBON CUP

ENGLISH POWERED WAY TO NEW PEAK

Nicholas English, who has played so many stirring games for Tipperary in senior hurling, stamped his personality in a big way during the 'Eighties, on the Universities' senior hurling championship for the Fitzgibbon Cup.

Between 1981 and 1985, inclusive, UCC set a new standard for title wins in succession by taking the Cup five seasons on the trot. English played in each of the five championship winning teams and also scored in all five finals. In 1984, Cork recorded a first four-in-a-row sequence in Fitzgibbon Cup history.

Cork went on to stretch their record of championship wins in succession to eight in 1988. English did not play in any of the games after 1985, but, even so, his record in the championship is still remarkable.

UCD were the first winners of the Fitzgibbon Cup in 1912. Cork took the second championship, and Galway joined the winning rankings in 1919.

Surprisingly enough, Queen's University won out in the series long before they made their title breakthrough in football. The Northern University were champions in 1953, and that success remains their only one.

St Patrick's, Maynooth, made it into the winners' ranking in double-quick style. After setting out on the trail in 1972, they won out in 1973. The newcomers beat UCG by 2-12 to 4-4 at Galway.

Paudie Fitzmaurice (Limerick) scored five points in the final to finish top scorer with 0-16 in two games. He was outshone in the scoring parade in the summit, however, by team-mate Henry Goff, who helped himself to a brace of goals.

Centre half back Seán Silke (Galway), Andy Fenton (Galway) at midfield and Seán Stack (Clare) in attack were others who played major roles in shaping history for Maynooth.

Maynooth retained the title the following season when Fitzmaurice again finished the leading scorer with 1-15 in three games. The Kildare University has not won the crown in the meantime.

Cork's great run of eight titles in a row ended in 1989 when they went down in a semi-final to UCD in Dublin by 1-12 to 0-9. By then, the field for the Fitzgibbon had been further widened, and the other semi-final featured Waterford Regional Technical College and NIHE, Limerick.

NIHE won that semi-final by 2-13 to 0-3.

They made history on the double with a final win over UCD, thanks to a late goal by Eoin Cleary.

The teams were level at 1-9 each two minutes from the end. Then up popped Cleary to send to the net for a dramatic winner that closed the scoring.

NIHE, as well as capturing their first title on their debut in a summit, became the first non-university side to take the Fitzgibbon Cup.

Waterford RTC had not long to wait

Nicholas English ... a new peak with UCC

after that 1989 semi-final for their entry into the Cup winners rankings. Noel Ryan, son of former referee of the same name, proved the inspiration of their 1-19 to 1-8 win over University of Limerick at the Gaelic Grounds in 1992.

Dalton had a capital game at right full forward and finished with 0-10 to his credit. Pádraig Fanning captained the side in impressive style from centre half forward and midfielders Donnacha O'Donnell and Owen Cummins were others to shine for the Waterford side.

The Fitzgibbon Cup championship commenced one year after the Sigerson Cup. The trophy was presented by the Rev Dr Edwin Fitzgibbon, OFM, a native of Dungourney and Professor of Philosophy at the time in UCC.

ROLL OF HONOUR

35	University College, Cork	1913,	1914,	1918,	1920,	1922,
		1925,	1928,	1929,	1930,	1933,
		1937,	1939,	1940,	1943,	1947,
		1955,	1956,	1958,	1961,	1962,
		1966,	1967,	1971,	1972,	1976,
		1981,	1982,	1983,	1984,	1985,
		1986,	1987,	1988,	1990,	1991.
31	University College, Dublin	1912,	1915,	1916,	1917,	1923,
		1924,	1927,	1931,	1932,	1934,
		1935,	1936,	1938,	1941,	1944,
		1948,	1950,	1951,	1952,	1957,
		1959,	1960,	1963,	1964,	1965,
		1968,	1969,	1975,	1978,	1979,
		1993.				
10	University College, Galway	1919,	1926,	1942,	1945,	1946,
		1949,	1954,	1970,	1977,	1980.
2	St Patrick's Maynooth	1973,	1974.			
	NIHE, Limerick*	1989,	1994.			
	Waterford RTC	1992,	1995.			
1	Queen's, Belfast	1953.				

Note: No competition in 1921.

*   now University of Limerick

65

Vocational Schools

This is the record of the various counties in the All-Ireland Vocational Schools Hurling and Football championships.

Hurling

12	Galway	1980,	1981,	1982,	1983,	1984,
		1985,	1986,	1987,	1992,	1993,
		1994,	1995.			
9	North Tipperary	1962,	1964,	1965,	1966,	1967,
		1968,	1969,	1974,	1978.	
8	Kilkenny	1963,	1972,	1973,	1975,	1976,
		1977,	1989,	1991.		
2	Tipperary	1988,	1990.			
1	Limerick City	1961.				
	Cork County	1970.				
	Antrim	1971.				
	Clare	1979.				

Football

8	Kerry	1973,	1977,	1978,	1986,	1987,
		1990,	1992,	1993.		
5	Tyrone	1967,	1969,	1970,	1988,	1989.
3	Derry	1979,	1980,	1981.		
	Donegal	1984,	1985,	1995.		
	Galway	1964,	1965,	1976.		
	Mayo	1971,	1975,	1982.		
2	Cork	1991,	1994.			
	Wicklow	1974,	1983.			
1	Fermanagh	1966.				
	Antrim	1968.				
	Carlow	1972.				
	Cork City	1961.				

GAMES ABROAD

EVERS SPARKLES AS
WEMBLEY STORY IS LAUNCHED

It will come as a surprise to many readers to learn that Wembley Stadium, London, so closely associated with major soccer games, was a venue for an annual Gaelic Games programme over as many as 19 years.

Not only that, the matches created such interest across the channel at times that some of the games during the period were televised live by British television.

Wembley's connection with Gaelic Games began in May 1958 with a double bill at senior level, featuring Galway and Derry in football and Kilkenny and Clare in hurling. The attendance was 33,240.

Midfielder Frank Evers was a bright star for Galway as they beat Derry by 3-9 to 2-5. The hurling game produced a feast of goals (11 in all), but the respective goalkeepers, Ollie Walsh, of Kilkenny, and Mick Hayes, Clare, still gave top class displays.

Sean Clohessy, Kilkenny's right full forward, helped himself to three goals to spearhead the Noreside win by 6-10 to 5-7.

Kilkenny's right half back, Paddy Buggy, was later President of the GAA.

Pat Kirby, Clare's right full forward, later carved out a tremendous reputation for himself as a handballer, both in Ireland and the US. He won the World singles title in 1970 when the championships were staged in Dublin to mark the official opening of the then new handball court in the capital.

However, Kirby represented the US that year. He was then resident in the US.

The largest attendance was in 1963, when the clashes of Kerry and Cavan in football, and Kilkenny and Tipperary in hurling, attracted a crowd of 42,500.

The matches were played in May up to 1976 and that year's matches went on in October. The programme involving Dublin and Kerry in football, and the hurlers of Cork and Wexford hurlers proved the last of the series.

High scoring achievements were accomplished by Paddy Barry (Cork) and Eddie Keher and Denis Heaslip (Kilkenny) in hurling and Mayo's Joe Corcoran, Bernie O'Callaghan (Kerry) and Tony McTague (Offaly) in football.

Barry scored 3-4 as Cork beat Kilkenny in 1959. Heaslip equalled that scoreline for Kilkenny in a win a year later over Waterford.

Eddie Keher (Kilkenny) scored 1-10 in 1973 against Tipperary, but he was playing for the All Stars. That year, the Carrolls All Stars provided the opposition to Kerry in football.

Joe Corcoran scaled new heights in football with 1-9 for Mayo as they saw off Meath in 1968. That improved on the earlier marker of 1-8 by Bernie O'Callaghan as Kerry beat Cavan in 1963.

Then, in 1973, McTague in the colours of the All Stars hit 1-8 in an unsuccessful bid by the national side against Kerry.

THE WINNERS LIST

HURLING

6	Cork	1959,	1966,	1967,	1970,	1971,	1976.
	Kilkenny	1958,	1960,	1963,	1965,	1974,	1975.
5	Tipperary	1961,	1962,	1964,	1969,	1972.	
1	All Stars	1973.					
	Wexford	1968.					

FOOTBALL

4	Down	1959,	1960,	1961,	1969.
	Galway	1958,	1964,	1974,	1975.
	Kerry	1962,	1963,	1971,	1973.
2	Cavan	1966,	1967.		
	Derry	1971,	1972.		
	Mayo	1968,	1970.		
1	Cork	1972.			
	Dublin	1976.			
	Meath	1965.			

NOTE: All the games were between inter-county teams, except in 1973, when All Stars selections competed in both codes. The All Stars footballers lost to Kerry and the hurlers beat Tipperary.

GAMES ABROAD

THE AUSTRALIAN CONNECTION

Ireland beat Australia in Australia in 1986 and 1990 in a Test series of international games under Compromise Rules. The boys in green were captained

Robbie O'Malley (Meath) ... led Ireland to victory "Down Under" in 1990

to those memorable triumphs by Jack O'Shea (Kerry) and Robbie O'Malley (Meath).

However, the story of these games really began in October 1967, when an Australian squad visited Ireland and had games with Meath and Mayo at Croke Park. The Australians beat the Royal County by 3-16 to 1-10 and the clash with Mayo was played on a Saturday and attracted a bumper attendance. The visitors won that encounter by 2-12 to 2-5.

In the spring of 1968, Meath visited Australia and played five games, winning them all.

The Australians visited Ireland again in the autumn of 1968, drew with Kerry at Killarney and beat the Combined Universities and Down at Croke Park.

Contacts continued in 1970 when Kerry went on a World Tour and Mick O'Dwyer celebrated with a scoring spectacular. He helped himself to 9-30 (57 points) in seven games at a splendid average of 8.14 points. Kerry visited Freemantle, Melbourne, Adelaide, Wagga Wagga, Sydney, Auckland and San Francisco and returned home with the perfect record from matches against a variety of opposition.

However, the Compromise Rules Test series did not begin until 1984, the GAA Centenary Year. The Australians won the opening match in Cork, lost to Ireland at Croke Park in the next round, but won the third and the series.

Then came Jack O'Shea's raiders' successful visit "down under" in 1986, when they came back from defeat in the opening match at Perth to level the series in Melbourne.

The third match in Adelaide was televised live to Ireland and, despite the morning showing time, attracted a tremendous viewing audience. The Irish rewarded followers at home with a power-packed display to win by 55 points to 32 points to clinch the series.

The final match was dominated by Ireland's full forward, John O'Driscoll (Cork), then only 19, who gave a five-star show as he belied his youth with play that had even Australian supporters applauding.

Australia took their revenge on their visit to Ireland in 1987, recovering from a losing start in the opening match at Croke Park, to win the two remaining ties.

The next Test Series was not played until 1990. Ireland won the opening match in Melbourne and clinched the title in their next game at Canberra with a 52-31 win. Jim Stynes, who won an All-Ireland minor football medal with Dublin in 1984 at midfield, but then went on to a successful career in Australian Rules football, lined out with Ireland. A former Ballyboden St Enda's club player, Stynes made a splendid contribution to the success, with a capital display highlighted by nine fine points.

Australia won the final match in Perth by 6 points, but by then, the Test title had been in safekeeping for the Irish. Australia won by 50 points to 44 points in what now ranks as the last chapter in this particular story of international games.

70

GAMES ABROAD

ENGLISH SHOOTS TO TOP IN TORONTO

The sharpshooting of Nicholas English helped to usher in a new but short era for Gaelic Games on a high note when the impressive Skydome in Toronto, home of the Blue Jays baseball team, echoed to the clash of the ash and the thud of an Irish football in a double bill of Gaelic Games on March 18, 1990.

English scored 2-4 as he helped Tipperary beat an All Stars selection in hurling by 5-15 to 3-11. Éanna Ryan (Galway) gave the All Stars the best possible start with a goal after only four minutes. Two minutes later, however, Cormac Bonner collected Tipperary's first goal and initiated a power show that carried the then All-Ireland champions to a convincing win.

Michael Cleary, who scored seven points, Donie O'Connell also in attack, and left full back Bobby Ryan were others to shine for Tipperary.

Éanna Ryan, who finished with 2-2, Joe Cooney (Galway), Jim Cashman (Cork) and Aidan Fogarty (Offaly) were best for the All Stars.

Dublin and Tyrone provided a closely contested and very competitive game in football. A goal by Vinny Murphy after about 44 minutes was the decisive score as the Dubs edged home by 1-8 to 0-10.

The respective goalkeepers, John O'Leary (Dublin) and Aidan Skelton, were in great form. Forward Paul Curran, Murphy and Barney Rock, who scored four points, of Dublin, and Peter Canavan, Sean McNally in attack and defender Sean Meyler of Tyrone, were among the leading lights of the history-making game.

Canavan scored four points.

The double bill attracted an attendance of 30,000 and was televised live to Ireland. There was also live TV coverage in Canada.

Chapter two, and the final chapter so far in this all too short a story, was written on St Patrick's Day 1991, when Cork, who had completed the rare double of All-Ireland senior titles in hurling and football the previous September, were doubly engaged.

The expert finishing of Colm O'Neill, who hit five points, did much to shape the Leesiders 1-12 to 1-9 win over the All Stars, in football.

Paul Staunton (Roscommon) kept a good goal for the All Stars and brought off a great save from Mick McCarthy four minutes into the second half.

Shea Fahy and Danny Culloty at midfield and Dave Barry, who goaled from a penalty, provided good support to O'Neill in the Cork side. James McCartan (Down), Jack O'Shea (Kerry) after going in as a substitute, and left full back Terry Ferguson (Meath), as well as Staunton, impressed for the All Stars.

In hurling, Cork were surprisingly trounced 5-13 to 0-6 by a splendid All Stars team, in which English was again to the fore with 1-2. Peter Finnerty (Galway), Tom Dempsey (Wexford) and Eamonn Morrissey (Kilkenny) were others who exercised important influences on the All Stars winning show.

English topped the scoring returns for the two seasons with that 2-4 in the opening round. O'Neill's five points put him on top of the football scoring review.

FITZGERALD OUTKICKS THE WORLD

Maurice Fitzgerald (Kerry) commands a special place in terms of achievements abroad by a Gaelic footballer. His feat, however, was recorded not in a team game, but in an individual competition, but was nonetheless of major importance for all that.

The inaugural World Kicking Championship was held in Melbourne in 1989 and Fitzgerald represented Ireland. He competed with players from American Football, Rugby League, Rugby Union, Soccer and Australian Rules football – competition of the highest class, it has to be admitted.

Maurice Fitzgerald ...
outkicked the world

However, Fitzgerald, from St Mary's, Cahirciveen, more than proved equal to the occasion. He out-kicked all comers, and did himself, Gaelic football and Ireland proud by emerging as the champion.

A wonderful distinction that for Fitzgerald and all the more noteworthy for the fact that, at that time, he was only about a year in senior inter-county football.

But then, top honours came quickly to Fitzgerald. He won his first Bank of Ireland All Star as right half forward in the 1988 team, only some months after collecting his second successive Munster under-21 medal.

Fitzgerald has been Kerry's most consistent marksman throughout his career with the county senior team.

Ladies Football

Mary Jo Curran – All Stars Specialist

Mary Jo Curran, of Kerry, enhanced a remarkable record in ladies football when she was chosen as centre half forward in the 1993 All Stars team. She won her eleventh such award and ranks as the only player chosen in every All Stars side since the inception of the awards. A truly wonderful achievement!

Mary Jo Curran collects another All Stars Trophy from Pat Quill of the Ladies Football Association

One of the most stylish players in the annals of the sport, Curran helped Kerry to regain the All-Ireland senior title in 1993 after an interval of three years. She gained her tenth senior medal.

This South Kerry player has distinguished herself at midfield and in attack during her wonderful career so far, and she has also won National League, inter-provincial and, of course, Munster medals.

Patricia Mimna made history on the double in 1993 when London beat Donegal to take the All-Ireland junior title for the first time. She captained the Exiles to that success.

Five years earlier, London were affiliated to the Central Council and also made their debut in an All-Ireland junior final. They were captained by Mimna in that game and lost to Leitrim.

However, Mimna was no stranger to All-Ireland final action when she lined out with London in that junior final of 1988. A native of Swanlinbar, she captained Cavan in their first appearance in an All-Ireland senior final in 1980. The Breffni girls lost by two points.

A year later Cavan, with Mimna again in their side, lost the showpiece game of the year to Offaly by a point.

Patricia went to London soon after that, took a two-year break from the game, then returned to football with Wembley Gaels in the British capital.

After leading London to their historic win, Mimna was named Player of the Junior Final and also chosen as an All Star. She earlier won two All Stars trophies with Cavan and one with London.

The first All-Ireland finals at Croke Park were played in 1986 when Waterford beat Wexford in the junior final and Kerry outscored Wexford in the senior.

The Kingdom won nine senior titles in a row from 1982 to 1990 inclusive, a record for the championship that is likely to stand for a long time to come. Marion O'Doherty captained Kerry to the 1982 title and is the only player to have played in every game in that great run.

No player captained Kerry more than once in that great unbeaten sequence.

The Ladies Association was founded at Hayes' Hotel, Thurles, in 1974, and the first All-Ireland senior championship was played that year. Tipperary were the initial champions and a year later completed the first All-Ireland senior titles double.

An under-16 championship was launched in 1976, club senior national test in 1977-78 and under-18 in 1980. The junior championship was launched in 1985.

The All-Ireland Senior Ranking

11	Kerry	1976,	1982,	1983,	1984,	1985,	1986,
		1987,	1988,	1989,	1990,	1993.	
4	Waterford	1991,	1992,	1994,	1995.		
3	Tipperary	1974,	1975,	1980.			
2	Offaly	1979,	1981.				
1	Cavan	1977.					
	Roscommon	1978.					

HANDBALL

MICHAEL WALSH – CHAMPION SUPREME

Michael "Duxie" Walsh confirmed his position as one of the all-time greats of Irish sport when he beat old rival Walter O'Connor (Meath) at Croke Park in September 1993 to become the first handballer to win nine All-Ireland senior softball singles championships in succession.

That was a tremendous achievement, one of the greatest ever, in fact, in any branch of Irish sport. The run was also a tribute not only to the exceptional skills of the Kilkenny stylist, but also to his commitment and consistency over such a lengthy period.

It takes something extra special to remain at the top over such a long span of years, but then Walsh has long since shown that he is a handballer apart.

He has been winning All-Ireland titles since his juvenile days almost as if they were going out of fashion. He won his first All-Ireland title in 1977, and has collected at least one national medal every year since then.

Walsh also made history as a teenager. An Irish side competed in the US Junior championships for the first time in 1981, and the Kilkenny ace took the

Michael Walsh (Kilkenny)
... Records galore

15 years and under championship. He was Ireland's only winner that year.

The dynamic Noresider won eight All-Ireland titles in the GAA Centenary year of 1984, including all six minor championships.

The Walsh-O'Connor 1993 softball decider was played before probably the biggest gallery ever at a handball match in this country. Walsh won the first tie in the Croke Park show-down by 21-8, lost the second 16-21 after leading by 12-3, but came back well to clinch the title by 21-15.

A year earlier, Michael Walsh equalled the long-standing record of eight All-Ireland senior championships established by the late Paddy Perry (Roscommon) between 1930 and 1937.

He was a giant of his era in the sport, and also excelled at hurling and football. He won Dublin county senior championship medals with Garda in each code.

Paddy Perry died in 1983. His widow was present at Croke Park on the night that Walsh equalled the Roscommon native's record, and again when "Duxie" wrote his name into the record books.

Then in September 1995, Walsh won his eleventh successive All-Ireland senior softball singles title.

MAHER – WORLD CHAMPION

Joey Maher (Louth) and the late Des Dillon, a native of Clare, but representing Dublin, ushered in a new era for handball when they competed in the World Championships in New York in 1964. Maher competed in singles and did well to finish in fourth place. He and Dillon finished fourth in the doubles..

Three years later, in the next World Championships in Toronto, Maher won the title – but in the Canadian singlet. He had been in residence for some years in Canada, and won the singles crown there in 1966 and 1967.

The Louth man beat Karl Obert (USA) in the final, and retained the Canadian singles crown in 1968. Later that year, he returned to Ireland and continued in the sport in this country where he left off in local competitions.

Maher had won All-Ireland titles before going to Canada, and he was back to national championship winning form after his return, so much so that he earned his place in the World Championships for the tests staged in Dublin in 1970 to mark the official opening of the then new glass court at Croke Park.

Maher qualified for the final, and came up against an Irish man, Pat Kirby, who, however, was representing the US. Kirby won 21-19, 21-12.

So, two Irish men won World titles in handball but ironically enough, not in the colours of their native land.

O'ROURKE STRIKES IT RICH FOR IRELAND

Tommy O'Rourke (Kildare) did make it a World title for Ireland when the World championships were staged in this country in 1984 to mark the GAA Centenary year celebrations. He won the 60 x 30 title in decisive fashion.

O'Rourke also helped to usher in a new era for the sport in this country as one of the first two Irish players to compete at under-22 in the US championships in 1978. He has a special place in Kildare handball as well because he brought the All-Ireland minor 60 x 30 softball singles crown to the county for the first time in expert fashion in 1963.

The Quish brothers, Tom and John, of Limerick, took the World doubles 60 x 30 championship at Dublin in Centenary Year.

DOUBLE FIRST FOR CURRAN

Ciaran Curran, one of the brightest young talents in handball in the country at present, has a proud double first to his credit at under-age level.

The Tyrone player celebrated his debut in the US Junior Championships in 1989 by winning the 15 years and under title to record the first title win in the tests by an Ulster handballer.

Curran won the 17 years and under title in 1990, made a successful defence of that championship a year later, and in 1992 took the 19 years and under crown. He thus became the first Irish handballer to win four US junior titles in succession in the under-age championships.

Curran went close to a fifth successive crown in 1993 when he lost the 19 years and under final in Illinois in a tie-breaker.

HISTORIC WIN BY MCCABE

Séamus McCabe did more than win an All-Ireland handball championship by taking the national senior softball singles title in 1966. Although Ulster players, including McCabe himself, had got among the All-Ireland medals in the junior ranks prior to that, the win by the Monaghan man was the first-ever by a Northern handballer in the premier grade.

McCabe, a left hander from Clones, went close to that historic break-through a year before his unique performance. He only required one ace in the fourth game of his 1965 senior hardball singles final with Peadar McGee (Mayo) to take the title, but failed to get it and the Westerner eventually came out on top.

However, the Monaghan man made no mistake when the pair met in the softball final at Ballymote, Co. Sligo, in September 1966. McCabe retained the All-Ireland softball singles title in 1967 and later qualified for a place in Ireland's team for the second World championships in Toronto.

WORLD DOUBLES CROWN

Dick Lyng and Séamus Buggy, of Wexford, brought a world doubles title to Ireland in 1970. They had a wonderful season, taking the All-Ireland senior softball doubles crown.

They were the country's representatives in the doubles championships in the World tests in Dublin in 1970. The Wexford pair beat combinations from Canada, Australia, Mexico and the US to emerge as champions.

John Ryan, of Wexford, was the first winner of the Gael-Linn Cup, a national winter competition which was introduced in 1953-54.

John Joe Gilmartin, from Talbot's Inch, had a truly memorable career, and won no fewer than 25 All-Ireland titles. He excelled at hardball and held the All-Ireland senior crown without a break from 1936 to 1942 inclusive – seven successive championships. He also played on five national doubles title winning teams in hardball during that period. He won two All-Ireland singles softball championships and three doubles between 1938 and 1941.

Gilmartin later spent some time in England where he suffered a shoulder injury. But following his return to Ireland, he regained the national senior hardball singles title in 1945 and collected a national doubles medal as well.

There was no softball championship in 1945, due to the scarcity of rubber at the time – World War II was just coming to an end then. The series was resumed in 1946. Gilmartin won the singles crown that year, and in hardball took four national titles – 1945 and 1947 singles and doubles.

DOUBLE FOR O'CONNOR

Walter O'Connor (Meath) ...
first Irish Open winner

Walter O'Connor blazed an impressive trail on the double in the titles-winning trail in 1992. He emerged from an entry of sixty as the winner of the inaugural Irish Open 40 x 20 singles championship. The Meath man beat Peter McAuley (Louth) in the final by 31-10.

Later in the year O'Connor was Meath's first ever All-Ireland senior 40 x 20 singles titlewinner, by beating Eddie Corbett (Tipperary) by 21-17, 15-21, 21-9 at St Coman's, Roscommon.

SECOND TIME LUCKY FOR KANE

It was a case of second time lucky for Kenneth Kane, a bright young handball prospect from Carlow, in the US Junior Championships at Des Plaines, Illinois, at the end of 1993. Kane made an impressive debut in the championships at 15 years and under at Cincinnati in 1992 when he was beaten only in a tie-breaker in the semi-final by the eventual winner.

The Carlow youth was eligible again for the 15 years and under grade in Illinois, and went all the way to the top. In fact, it proved a successful grade for Ireland, as Kane's opponent in the decider was Tony Healy (Cork). The win in two sets by Kane also earned him a place in Carlow handball as the county's first US champion.

ALL STARS FOOTBALL

TREND SETTERS FROM DERRY

John McGurk, Henry Downey and Gary Coleman saw out 1993 on a high note by adding another unique chapter to an historic season for themselves and Derry in senior inter-county football.

All three joined the ranks of All Stars award winners for the first time. The gifted Derry trio also made up the entire half back line of the national squad, and earned the Oak Leaf county ranking as the first to provide the entire half back line in the history of the All Stars promotion.

Pat Spillane (Kerry) ... Record number of football All Stars

Derry also gained their best-ever representation with seven of their first All-Ireland title winning team honoured.

Another history-maker in the 1993 team was Kevin O'Neill (Mayo) who set the seal on his first season in the premier inter-county ranks by winning the right half forward berth. He is son of Liam O'Neill, a former Galway senior footballer, who won an All Star at right half back in 1973.

Kevin became the first son of a former All Star to join the exclusive company of footballers.

Anthony Tohill and Brian McGilligan, who did so much in spearheading Derry to their first-ever Sam Maguire Cup win in 1993, did not make history when paired at midfield in the All Stars side that season. Nonetheless, they still earned a rare enough ranking, as they became the first combination from the same county to man midfield since Jack O'Shea and Sean Walsh (Kerry) in 1981. They earned the Kingdom a first that year.

The All Stars awards were first presented in 1971. Right full forward in that team was Andy McCallin and he remains Antrim's solitary representative in the football rankings.

Anthony McGurk (Derry) was the first footballer to be honoured both as a forward and a defender. He was first chosen at left full forward in 1973, and then in 1975 won his only other award at centre half back.

Paddy Moriarty equalled that feat in 1977, and, amazingly enough, he completed exactly a similar double to McGurk. Moriarty won his first award in 1972 at No. 15 and also became Armagh's first representative in the rankings. He returned to favour in 1977 as pivot.

Pat Spillane won his first award in 1976 at left full forward. The Kerry man went on to collect his ninth trophy in 1986 and this ranks as the record number of wins by any footballer.

Séamus Clancy became Clare's first – and so far only – award winner when named at right full back in the 1992 team. The Banner County's place in the review brought the number of counties represented in the All Stars chart to twenty three.

Brian Murphy is the only player to gain selection in football AFTER winning an All-Ireland senior hurling medal the previous September. That distinction came the way of the talented Cork dual star in 1976 at left full back.

Eugene Mulligan (Offaly) was the first player to go into a team as a unanimous selection. He was chosen at right half back in the inaugural football side of 1971.

Paddy Cullen (Dublin) and Martin Furlong (Offaly) set the pace for goalkeepers with four awards each.

Donie O'Sullivan was the first Kerry man honoured. Indeed, the Kingdom defender, named at left full back in 1971, was, surprisingly enough, one of only two Kerry men honoured over the first two years of the promotion.

Ger Houlahan ended an eleven year wait for Armagh when named as full forward in the 1993 team. Prior to his selection, Joe Kernan ranked as the last footballer from the Orchard County to gain selection. He was centre half forward in the 1982 team.

ALL STARS HURLING

STOREY AND DUNNE
BRIGHTEN YEAR FOR WEXFORD

The 1993 hurling season promised so much for Wexford but yielded nothing in terms of major titles. The county lost to Cork after two replays in the National League final, and went down to Kilkenny in the Leinster final after a replay.

However, Martin Storey and Liam Dunne helped to brighten the year in the dark days of December with their inclusion in the All Stars team. This was the county's best representation since as far back as 1977 – a surprising statistic that for Wexford, whose teams provided so many golden moments in the game throughout the 'Eighties and in the early years of the 'Nineties.

Ciaran Barr (Antrim) ... a first hurling winner from Ulster

Dunne, chosen at right half back, won his second trophy. He was left half back in the 1990 team. Storey joined the ranks for the first time with his selection at right half forward.

It is an indication of the steadily improving standard in Ulster that the province was represented in the 1991, 1992 and 1993 teams. This run came after Ciarán Barr (Antrim) entered the ranks as the North's first All Star in 1988 as centre half forward.

Des Donnelly, left full back, and Olcan McFetridge, left half forward, both in 1989, increased Antrim's position in the review. The North was not represented in 1990.

Terence McNaughton at midfield was Antrim's and Ulster's

only standard-bearer in 1991. A year later, Gerard McGratten marched into the history books when he found favour at right half forward. He is the only Down hurler honoured so far.

Paul McKillen (Antrim) won his spurs at left midfield in 1993 to complete the Ulster story so far.

Pat Hartigan (Limerick) was full back in hurling each year from 1971 to 1975 inclusive, and the first outfield player to win five trophies in the same position.

Noel Skehan equalled that feat as a goalkeeper when he stepped up for his fifth award in 1976. The great Kilkenny custodian went on to win trophies in 1982 and 1983 and now ranks as the record-maker in hurling.

Ray Cummins (Cork) was the sole choice in hurling as full forward in 1972 – the first unanimous selection in the code. The following year, Pat Hartigan joined that exclusive company as the solitary nomination at full back.

Family connections ... Colm Doran was right half back in 1973, and his brother, Tony, collected another trophy for the family in 1976 at full forward.

Martin Quigley won four awards. In 1974, when he gained the second honour, his colleagues included brother John as right full forward. Martin was centre half forward.

The year 1983 proved a vintage one on the family connection story. John Henderson was right full back, while his brother Ger was honoured at centre half. The Fennelly brothers, Ger and Liam, were both in the attack, and this ranks as the only selection in which two sets of brothers found favour in the same year.

Long Wait

Brian McMahon ended a long, long wait for Dublin as the 1990 full forward. He became the first from the county to find favour since Mickey Bermingham held down the right full forward spot in the initial team back in 1971. No Dubliner has since won an All Stars trophy.

Tommy Quaid had to wait almost to the end of his career for a first All Star selection. He was 36 when he found favour as goalkeeper in 1992. He first played senior inter-county hurling with Limerick in 1975 and was a bright light in their goal from then, except for a season as a forward, until he retired before the start of the 1993 Munster championship.

Liam Fennelly, who became the first man to receive the new Liam McCarthy Cup as Kilkenny's captain in 1992, and Tony O'Sullivan had announced their retirement from inter-county fare when they were honoured in 1992 at full forward and left half forward, respectively.

O'Sullivan subsequently made a come-back in 1993 to the Cork team and won a League medal.

ALL STARS –
THE CHART LEADERS

SPILLANE AND SKEHAN
THE TRAIL BLAZERS

The following are the players who blaze the trails in football and hurling as far as trophy wins are concerned in the All Stars promotion.

FOOTBALL

9	Spillane, Pat (Kerry):	1976,	1977,	1978,	1979,	1980,
		1981,	1984,	1985,	1986.	
7	Sheehy, Michael (Kerry):	1976,	1978,	1979,	1981,	1982,
		1984,	1986.			
6	O'Shea, Jack (Kerry):	1980,	1981,	1982,	1983,	1984,
		1985.				
	Power, Ger (Kerry):	1975,	1976,	1978,	1979,	1980,
		1986.				
5	Egan, John (Kerry):	1975,	1977,	1978,	1980,	1982.
	O'Keeffe, John (Kerry):	1973,	1975,	1976,	1978,	1979.
	Ó Séa, Padi (Kerry):	1981,	1982,	1983,	1984,	1985.
4	Cullen, Paddy (Dublin):	1974,	1976,	1977,	1979.	
	Drumm, Tommy (Dublin):	1977,	1978,	1979,	1983.	
	Furlong, Martin (Offaly):	1972,	1981,	1982,	1983.	
	Kelleher, Robbie (Dublin):	1974,	1975,	1977,	1978.	
	Liston, Eoin (Kerry):	1980,	1981,	1982,	1984.	
	O'Leary, John Dublin):	1984,	1985,	1993,	1994.	

HURLING

7	Skehan, Noel (Kilkenny):	1972,	1973,	1974,	1975,	1976,
		1982,	1983.			

6	McKenna, Joe (Limerick):	1974,	1975,	1978,	1979,	1980, 1981.
6	English, Nicholas (Tipperary):	1983,	1984,	1985,	1987,	1988, 1989.
5	Cooney, Joe (Galway):	1985,	1986,	1987,	1989,	1990.
	Fenton, John (Cork):	1983,	1984,	1985,	1986,	1987.
	Finnerty, Peter (Galway):	1985,	1986,	1987,	1988,	1990.
	Hartigan, Pat (Kilkenny):	1971,	1972,	1973,	1974,	1975.
	Henderson, Ger (Kilkenny):	1978,	1979,	1982,	1983,	1987.
	Hennessy, Joe (Kilkenny):	1978,	1979,	1983,	1984,	1987.
	Keher, Eddie (Kilkenny):	1971,	1972,	1973,	1974,	1975.
	Barry-Murphy, Jimmy (Cork):	1976,	1977,	1978,	1983,	1986.
4	Carey, D.J. (Kilkenny):	1991,	1992,	1993,	1994.	
	Clarke, Iggy (Galway):	1975,	1978,	1979,	1980.	
	Cleary, Michael (Tipperary):	1990,	1991,	1992,	1993.	
	Coughlan, Denis (Cork):	1972,	1976,	1977,	1978.	
	Cummins, Frank (Kilkenny):	1971,	1972,	1982,	1983.	
	Cunningham, Ger (Cork):	1984,	1985,	1986,	1990.	
	Larkin, Phil "Fan" (Kilkenny):	1973,	1974,	1976,	1978.	
	O'Brien, Liam (Kilkenny):	1973,	1974,	1975,	1979.	
	O'Sullivan, Tony (Cork):	1986,	1988,	1990,	1992.	
	Quigley, Martin (Wexford):	1973,	1974,	1975,	1976.	

PLAYERS HONOURED IN BOTH CODES

Jimmy Barry-Murphy, who played so many excellent games for Cork in football and hurling and won All-Ireland medals in both codes, is the record-maker in the review of players who have won All Stars awards in football and hurling.

7	Barry-Murphy, Jimmy (Cork):	Hurling:	1976, 1977, 1978, 1983, 1986.
		Football:	1973, 1974.
5	Cummins, Ray (Cork):	Hurling:	1971, 1972, 1977.
		Football:	1971, 1973.
4	Murphy, Brian (Cork):	Hurling:	1979, 1981.
		Football:	1973, 1976.
2	Currams, Liam (Offaly):	Hurling:	1981.
		Football:	1982.

All-Ireland Club Championships

A Special Double For Pakie Cooney

Pakie Cooney has special reasons for recalling the national festivals of 1993 and 1994. He captained Sarsfields of Galway to their first All-Ireland club senior hurling title on St Patrick's Day 1993, in a final win over Kilmallock, Limerick, when he held down the right full back position at Croke Park.

Sarsfields were back at headquarters on St Patrick's Day 1994 for the final defence of the AIB national title against final newcomers Toomevara, Tipperary. Cooney was again their captain and right full back.

The Galway club became the first to appear in a hurling final as defending All-Ireland champions and they went a step further by retaining the title.

Aidan Donohue was joint top scorer with Peter Cooney in the final win of 1993. He scored 0-5 and Cooney hit 1-2.

Donohue was out on his own in the scoring stakes in 1994 in the win over Toomevara. He turned in a Man-of-the-Match performance as he slotted over nine golden points in the two points Sarsfields success.

Jimmy Kerrigan and Timmy Dalton enhanced their positions on top of the All-Ireland medal winners rankings for club football championship by helping Nemo Rangers in 1994 to regain the title after an interval of five years.

Kerrigan and Dalton were team-mates in the Cork club's earlier final wins of 1979, 1982, 1984 and 1989. They boosted their collections of medals, then, to an impressive five in the 1994 win over final newcomers Castlebar Mitchells, Mayo, at Croke Park. As a result, the Cork pair head the All-Ireland medals rankings for the competition. Joint second are Brian Murphy and Dinny Allen, both of Nemo, with four medals.

Michael McCarthy was not the first Cork man to captain an All-Ireland club senior football title winning team when he led O'Donovan Rossa, Skibbereen, to the 1993 title. Even so, he still earned a special ranking as far as successful Rebel County team leaders are concerned.

O'Donovan Rossa are the only Cork club from outside Cork city to win the title. McCarthy earned another proud distinction during the campaign by scoring 1-8 when he made a mighty contribution in earning his side a draw with Éire Óg, Carlow, in the final at Croke Park.

That score sent the Skibbereen man powering to the top of the individual scoring chart for football finals, to join another Cork native, Eoin O'Mahony, in the premier position.

He helped himself to 1-8 for Nemo Rangers in their win over Clan na nGael, of Roscommon, at Croke Park in 1989.

McCarthy was a consistent sharpshooter with O'Donovan Rossa throughout the glory campaign. He was the only player in the side to score in every game and headed the club's chart with 3-33 (42 points) in six outings, or seven points a game on average.

The gifted full forward had his best match score of the campaign in the semi-final against Lavey, of Derry, at Ballinascreen, where he notched 1-9.

Back to the Sarsfields double in hurling. The Cooney brothers, Pakie, Brendan and Michael in defence, Joe at midfield and Peter in attack were all to the fore in the two title wins.

Interestingly enough, the Castlegar (Galway) side that brought the All-Ireland hurling title to the West for the first time in 1980 included five Connolly brothers. Pádraig was full back, John held down the No. 6 spot, Joe, Gerry and Michael all played in attack in the team that beat Ballycastle, of Antrim, at Navan. Not only that, Michael captained the side from the full forward.

No Galway club won the title again until Kiltormer came out on top in 1992. A year later came that Sarsfields win already detailed and that was also the first time clubs from the Connacht stronghold won the title in successive years.

In sharp contrast to the hurling success story, the West has still to provide a winner of the football crown.

The club championships have gone from success to success since they were launched in the 1970-71 season. They now arouse tremendous interest and all games are very well supported.

East Kerry beat Bryansford, of Down, in the first football final. That Kerry side was a divisional selection, but such teams are no longer allowed to compete in the championships. Colleges and Universities' teams are also now ineligible.

Michael Gleeson, then an inter-county footballer, led the Kerry side to victory in the inaugural football summit on November 21, 1971, at Croke Park and was presented with the All-Ireland club shield. He also scored 2-1 to emerge as the leading marksman in the final.

The first official hurling final was played at Birr on December 19, 1971 and resulted in another first for Munster in the story of All-Ireland finals.

Roscrea, of Tipperary, beat St. Rynagh's of Offaly, and J Tynan, of the Southern champions, headed the scoring return with 2-0.

There was a change of trophy in football for the winners during 1974. UC Dublin beat Clan na nGael of Lurgan, in a replay at Croke Park. Fr Michael Kitt, then chairman of the Castletown club in Wexford, presented the Andy Merrigan Cup to the then president of the GAA, Dr Donal Keenan. He, in turn, presented the trophy to Paddy Kerr of Monaghan, the UCD left half back and captain.

The trophy commemorates the late Andy Merrigan, a former playing member of the Castletown club, who also played with the Wexford senior football team. He died at the height of his playing career following a farming accident.

The student side retained the title in 1975 to complete the first run of two successive All-Ireland titles in the code.

The winners of the senior hurling title now receive the Tommy Moore Cup. This trophy commemorates Tommy Moore, who was a legendary figure in hurling with Faughs and Dublin.

He won two All-Ireland senior hurling medals and four Leinster senior medals with the county, as well as six Dublin senior souvenirs with Faughs.

Faughs presented the Tommy Moore Cup in memory of their former hurling giant and long-time club man.

Cork clubs dominated the hurling series during the 'Seventies. Blackrock won three titles, Glen Rovers and St Finbarr's two each. Indeed, between 1972 and 1979 inclusive, Leeside clubs won the title each year except in 1976.

Surprisingly, after that great start, only one Cork club, Midleton in 1988, has captured the national crown.

Cork also set the pace in football. Nemo Rangers have won more titles than any other club, a total of six. St Finbarr's come next with three crowns, and also rank as the only club to win All-Ireland titles in hurling and football.

THE CHAMPIONS LINE-UP
HURLING

3	Blackrock, Cork:	1972,	1974,	1979.
	Shamrocks, Kilkenny:	1981,	1984,	1990.
2	Glen Rovers, Cork:	1973,	1977.	
	James Stephens, Kilkenny:	1976	1982.	
	Sarsfields, Galway:	1993,	1994.	
	St Finbarr's, Cork:	1975,	1978.	
1	Birr, Offaly:	1995.		
	Borris-Ileigh, Tipperary:	1987.		
	Buffer's Alley, Wexford:	1989.		
	Castlegar, Galway:	1980.		
	Glenmore, Kilkenny:	1991.		
	Kilruane McDonagh's, Tipperary:	1986.		
	Kiltormer, Galway:	1992.		
	Loughgiel Shamrocks, Antrim:	1983.		
	Midleton, Cork:	1988.		
	Roscrea, Tipperary:	1971.		
	St Martin's, Kilkenny:	1985.		

FOOTBALL

6	Nemo Rangers, Cork:	1973,	1979,	1982, 1984,
		1989,	1994.	
3	St Finbarr's, Cork:	1980,	1981,	1987.
2	Burren, Down:	1986,	1988.	
	UC, Dublin:	1974,	1975.	
1	Austin Stacks, Tralee:	1977.		
	Baltinglass, Wicklow:	1990.		
	Bellaghy, Derry:	1972.		
	Castleisland Desmonds, Kerry:	1985.		
	Dr Crokes, Killarney:	1992.		
	East Kerry:	1971.		
	Kilmacud Crokes, Dublin:	1995.		
	Lavey, Derry:	1991.		
	O'Donovan Rossa, Skibbereen:	1993.		
	Portlaoise:	1983.		
	St Vincent's, Dublin:	1976.		
	Thomond College, Limerick:	1978.		

Billy Morgan ... receives the Cup from the late PA "Weeshie" Murphy, then Munster Council Chairman, after leading Nemo Rangers, Cork, to their first All-Ireland club football title in 1973.

ALL-IRELAND UNDER-21 FOOTBALL

CANAVAN A RECORD-MAKER WITH THE SCORING TOUCH

It is not often that a forward scores 2-5 in an All-Ireland final. Rarer still that a player enhances such a first-rate achievement by leading his county as well to a first national triumph.

That was the double distinction achieved by Peter Canavan as he captained Tyrone to victory over Kerry at Newbridge in the 1991 All-Ireland under-21 football summit. That was only the Ulster county's second appearance in a national decider in the grade. A year earlier they were trounced by Kerry by 5-12 to 2-11 at Mullingar, a game in which Canavan scored 2-3.

Tyrone took a handsome revenge for their 1990 set-back by trouncing the Kingdom by 4-16 to 1-5 in the 1992 summit.

A year later, the O'Neill County, again captained by Canavan, were back in the final. They beat Galway at Longford to record the only double by an Ulster side and Canavan earned further mention in the record chart by becoming the first to captain two All-Ireland under-21 football title winning teams.

Meath made history on the double in 1993. They were without an All-Ireland semi-final win after four attempts when they lined out against Derry at Castleblayney in early August. The Royal County had to settle for a draw as Eamonn Burns scored the equalising point for the Ulster men a minute from the final whistle.

A week later, however, Meath finally made the long-awaited breakthrough when they won the replay at the same venue by two points.

If that first semi-final win was a long-time coming (Meath made their semi-final debut in 1985), the Royal County stars made no mistake in the decider against Kerry at Portlaoise.

A solid defence, powered by Graham Geraghty, Enda McManus and Thomas Hanley, hard-working midfielders Jimmy McGuinness and Tony Byrne and the accuracy of Cathal Sheridan who scored four points, proved the platform for a hard-earned but well-merited 1-8 to 0-10 in a thrilling encounter before 10,000 spectators. Thomas Hanley, left half back, joined the ranks of title winning captains.

There was an attendance of 10,497 at the first All-Ireland under-21 football final at Croke Park on September 13, 1964, when Kerry beat Laois by 1-10 to 1-3.

Kildare beat Cork in a classic game in 1965 and Roscommon outscored Kildare for the 1966 title.

Derry became the first Ulster county to appear in a decider in 1968. They had a winning debut as well, beating Offaly, who were also appearing in their initial decider, by two goals. So, the title was brought to each province over a five year period.

Kerry became the first county to win three titles in succession (1975 to 1977 inclusive). Charlie Nelligan, Michael Spillane, Jack O'Shea and Denis "Ogie" Moran each won a third successive medal in 1977.

The first drawn game was between Mayo and Kerry in 1967 at Croke Park. Mayo won the replay by 4-9 to 1-7 at Ballinasloe.

BILLY O'SULLIVAN TOPS SCORING CHART

Billy O'Sullivan established a new individual scoring record for a football final when he chalked up a majestic 4-1 for Kerry in a resounding win over Tyrone in 1991 at Cusack Park, Mullingar.

That improved by a point the long-standing record set early in the series by Willie McGee of Mayo. He scored 4-0 against Kerry in a final replay at Ballinasloe in 1967.

The leading individual returns in under-21 football finals are:

POINTS	SCORE	
13	4-1	Billy O'Sullivan (Kerry) v. Tyrone at Mullingar, 1990.
12	4-0	Willie McGee (Mayo) v. Kerry at Ballinasloe, replay 1967.
11	1-8	Gay Grehan (Offaly) v. Derry at Croke Park, 1968.
	2-5	Peter Canavan (Tyrone) v. Kerry at Newbridge, 1991.
10	1-7	Paul McGrath (Cork) v. Offaly at Thurles, 1986.
	1-7	Manus Boyle (Donegal) v. Kerry at Roscommon, replay, 1987.
9	1-6	Michael Sheehy (Kerry) v. Dublin at Tipperary Town, 1975.
	2-3	Peter Canavan (Tyrone) v. Kerry at Mullingar, 1990.

THE ALL-IRELAND RANKINGS

9	Cork	1970,	1971,	1980,	1981,	1984,	1985,
		1986,	1989,	1994.			
7	Kerry	1964,	1973,	1975,	1976,	1977,	1990,
		1995.					
3	Mayo	1967,	1974,	1983.			
2	Donegal	1982,	1987.				
	Roscommon	1966,	1978.				
	Tyrone	1991,	1992.				
1	Antrim	1969.					
	Derry	1968.					
	Down	1979.					
	Galway	1972.					
	Kildare	1965.					
	Meath	1993.					
	Offaly	1988.					

Niall Cahalane . . . who won All-Ireland Under-21 medal with Cork in 1984.

ALL-IRELAND UNDER-21 HURLING

TONY BROWNE,
A WATERFORD HISTORY-MAKER

Tony Browne and Seán Daly command special places in Waterford hurling. Browne joined the county's small list of All-Ireland title winning captains when he led a gifted under-21 side to victory over Offaly in a replay in 1992 at Kilkenny for Waterford's first national championship in the grade.

Browne, from Mount Sion, was an outstanding leader and right half back.

Daly proved the sharpshooter supreme in the glory run. He scored 6-10 (28 points) in five games, or 5.60 points a match on average. His best return in a single game was recorded at the expense of Antrim at Parnell Park, Dublin, where he shot a thundering 3-4 in an All-Ireland semi-final.

Paul Flynn scored five points in the replay to bring his total to 1-5 for the series. He also played with the minor side in 1993 and rifled over two points in the unsuccessful All-Ireland final bid against Galway some weeks earlier.

Flynn, from the Ballygunner club, is the only Waterford hurler to score in two All-Ireland finals in the same year.

Waterford became only the seventh county to win this title as a result of the 1992 triumph.

Tiipperary and Wexford ushered in the All-Ireland under-21 hurling final era when they met at Nowlan Park on October 4, 1964. The first half was evenly enough contested, but Tipperary pulled away in the second for a runaway 8-9 to 3-1.

Michael "Babs" Keating, better known in latter years as Tipperary team manager, captured the scoring spotlight by leading the returns for both teams with 2-3.

Wexford took revenge over Tipperary a year later in the final, but have not won the All-Ireland crown in the meantime.

The 1966 championship resulted in a remarkable series of three meetings between Cork and Wexford for the title. The first match at Kilkenny was a memorable one. Then the counties met at Limerick, where another fine game resulted in the first replay draw at that stage of any All-Ireland championship since 1931, when Cork and Kilkenny had three meetings before deciding the destination of the Liam McCarthy Cup.

The second replay at Croke Park did not match the earlier games for sustained excitement and high thrills, but it still had many bright moments, with Cork eventually coming out on top.

Cork were captained by Gerald McCarthy, who was also Cork's captain when they beat Kilkenny in the All-Ireland senior final the previous September. He thus joined the ranks of record-makers as the first man to skipper senior and under-21 title winning teams in All-Ireland championships in the same year.

Galway brought the title to Connacht for the first time in 1972 and in 1993 beat Kilkenny in a replay to capture their sixth title. Liam Burke, who played against Kilkenny in the unsuccessful Liam McCarthy Cup bid a few weeks earlier, led Galway to victory in fine style from midfield.

An Ulster county has yet to contest a national final.

Long-Standing Scoring Record

The individual scoring record for an All-Ireland under-21 hurling final is a long-standing one, having been established in the early years of the championship by Bernard Meade. He struck it rich in a big way for Cork in a 1968 win over Kilkenny at Waterford, where he made an outstanding contribution to his team's success by scoring 1-12.

The leading returns are:

Points Score

15	1-12	Bernard Meade (Cork) v. Kilkenny at Waterford, 1968.
14	2-8	Seán Barry (Cork) v. Wexford at Limerick, first draw, 1966.
13	1-10	Mick Butler (Wexford) v. Cork at Croke Park, draw, 1970.
	2-7	Connie Kelly (Cork) v. Wexford at Croke Park, replay, 1970.
12	4-0	John Rothwell (Cork) v. Wexford at Croke Park, 1971.

Roll of Honour

9	Cork	1966,	1968,	1969,	1970,	1971,	1973,
		1976,	1982,	1988.			
8	Tipperary	1964,	1967,	1979,	1980,	1981,	1985,
		1989,	1995.				
6	Galway	1972,	1978,	1983,	1986,	1991,	1993.
	Kilkenny	1974,	1975,	1977,	1984,	1990,	1994.
1	Limerick	1987.					
	Waterford	1992.					
	Wexford	1965.					

Railway Cups

Tony Scullion
An Interprovincial Footballer Apart

Tony Scullion walked proudly into Railway Cup football history on March 6, 1994, when he helped Ulster beat Munster at Ennis to complete the first-ever sequence of five interprovincial titles in succession in the code. The Derry man played in every one of the ten games on the way to that record by the North – the only player to achieve such a distinction.

Scullion was chosen at left full back for every game and had not to retire once during a match. He also joined the ranks of title-winning captains during the run, as he led the province to the 1991 championship.

The consistently high standard of football produced by the Ballinascreen man in the Ulster colours is further emphasised by the fact that he held the left full back position from 1987 without a break, up to and including the record making win. The 1994 decider proved a case of "Lucky 13" for Tony Scullion! That was his 13th appearance for Ulster.

Ulster regained the Railway Cup in 1989 after a five year interval. No competition was played in 1990 and Ulster resumed the campaign with a win at Ballybofey in March 1991 at the expense of Connacht.

Martin McQuillan, of Armagh, played in all but one of the ten games. He missed the 1993 semi-final against Munster at Newry.

McQuillan was right half back in all his engagements except the 1991 semi-final win over Connacht, when he wore the No. 7 jersey. He scored a goal in the 1991 final against Munster.

Brian McGilligan, who led Ulster to victory in the final game of the record series, takes third position in terms of outings. He played in eight games. He was not engaged in the 1989 championship, played in two games in 1991 and in the 1992 semi-final. He went in as a substitute in the final that year and retained his position for each of the remaining ties.

Ulster called on four goalkeepers: Paddy Linden (Monaghan), the two 1989 games, Garry Walsh (Donegal), both matches in 1991, Neil Collins (Down), the two matches in 1992, and Damien McCusker (Derry), the net-minder for the last four encounters.

Ulster's first win in the record-making run was featured by a remarkable scoring *tour-de-force* by their left full forward, Jim McConville. He helped himself to a thundering 4-3 in a win over Connacht at Mitchelstown to establish a new record for interprovincial football.

Prior to that, John Timmons (Dublin) had blazed the way with 1-10 for Leinster in a semi-final win over Munster at Tullamore in 1962. Some ten years later, Michael Kearins (Sligo) rifled over 0-13 as Connacht beat the Combined Universities in a quarter final tie at Roscommon.

Not surprisingly, McConville proved one of the leading scorers for the North over the series as a whole, even though he played in only three games. He chalked up 5-4.

Anthony Tohill joined McConville on top of the chart by scoring 0-2 at Ennis in the 1994 summit. That boosted his record to 2-13 from five games.

Peter Canavan grabbed the goal that really turned the key in the door for Ulster in the fifth final in the second half. He also scored a point to bring his record for the series to 2-12. The Tyrone man only went into the 1994 final as a substitute, and that limited outing marked his fourth appearance of the campaign.

THE RECORD RUN

This was how Ulster established the new record in Railway Cup football:

1989:	October 7	Mitchelstown: Ulster 4-8; Connacht 0-7.
	October 8	Páirc Uí Chaoimh: Ulster 1-11; Munster 1-8.
1991:	March 24	Ballybofey: Ulster 1-15; Connacht 1-13, after extra time.
	April 7	Croke Park: Ulster 1-11; Munster 1-8.
1992:	March 1	Carrick-on-Shannon: Ulster 0-11; Connacht 0-7.
	March 15	Newry: Ulster 2-7; Munster 0-8.
1993:	October 17	Newry: Ulster 3-17; Munster 0-8.
	October 31	Longford: Ulster 1-12; Leinster 0-12.
1994:	February 13	Armagh: Ulster 0-9; Leinster 1-5.
	March 6	Ennis: Ulster 1-6; Munster 1-4.

Ulster scored 14 goals and 107 points (149 points) and conceded 5-80 (95 points) over the ten game run.

Ulster became the first province to record nine consecutive wins in 1967 when they beat Leinster at Casement Park. The bid for a record five titles in a row was ended at Croke Park on St Patrick's Day when a Michael Kearins first goal set Connacht up for victory. The Sligo man found the net just before the interval.

Ulster went on in 1995 to stretch the record to six titles in a row with wins over Connacht (0-16 to 0-8) at Clones and Leinster (1-9 to 0-8) again at Clones. Scullion added to his earlier achievements by playing in each game at full back.

RING BLAZED AN AMAZING TRAIL

Christy Ring blazed an amazing trail in the Railway Cup in senior hurling. He had a tremendous span of service with his province stretching over 22 years, and his record of medal wins will never be remotely approached in the future, let alone surpassed.

The Cloyne native was first chosen by Munster as a substitute for the 1941 final with Leinster. A year later he made his debut in the side as centre half forward in the final against Leinster – Munster had a bye to that decider.

It was a winning debut and, from then on, Ring was an automatic choice for the South until the end of the 1963 series. That year he made his last appearance in the Munster blue in the final replay with Leinster, in which he had to retire with an injury after only 15 minutes play.

Ring made 44 appearances with Munster and scored 42 goals and 105 points (231 points). He failed to find the target in only three of his outings.

The first was the 1947 final, in which Connacht won the title for the first time; the second in the 1952 decider against Leinster, and the third on that limited appearance in the 1963 final replay.

The late legendary Cork man won 18 medals, naturally by far a record for hurling and football. He collected his awards from 1942 to 1946, inclusive, 1948 to 1953, 1955, 1957 to 1961, inclusive, and 1963.

Probably his greatest display for Munster was in the final of 1959 against Connacht, which was played in June to mark the official opening of what was then the new Hogan Stand at Croke Park.

With an exhibition of skill and dexterity, which he topped off with a great scoring total of 4-5, Ring was a glittering hero for the South. It was undoubtedly one of his finest hours and came at the age of 39. Truly remarkable!

O'NEILL SETS PACE IN FOOTBALL

Seán O'Neill (Down) sets the pace in football for interprovincial fare. He was chosen for every single Ulster team in the competition from the 1960 semi-final up to and including the 1974 semi-final, which the North lost.

The clever Down forward was then included among the substitutes for the 1975 semi-final, but later went into the match to help the North to victory over Connacht. He retained his place for the final.

He made 26 appearances in the saffron of Ulster, including the limited outing against the West in 1975, and ranks as the only man to win eight medals in football. His glory years were 1960, 1963, 1964, 1965, 1966, 1968, 1970 and 1971.

O'Neill scored 9-26 (53 points) for Ulster. In 1979, when Ulster regained the

Railway Cup after an interval of eight years, O'Neill played a major dual role as selector and trainer.

DOUBLE FOR DES

Des Foley walked into Railway Cup history in brilliant style in 1962 when he became the first to win interprovincial medals on the same afternoon.

The Dubliner turned in a power-packed performance at midfield for Leinster to spark a famous hurling win over Munster, who were chasing a sixth title in succession. Four separate Southern hurlers "marked" the Dubliner during the hour, but he was unbeatable. Leinster won by two points, and there could hardly be a better way to win a first interprovincial than the manner in which Foley dominated the exchanges.

After that game, Des Foley lined out with Leinster in the football final against Ulster. He had a good game as well, a tribute that to his class and dedication, as the East came out on top. He lined out at midfield.

As a result, Des Foley became the first player to win interprovincial medals in both codes on the same afternoon. He still ranks as the only man to hold such a distinction.

OVER THE BORDER

Kevin Armstrong, a dual player with Antrim and Ulster, brought the Railway Cup football trophy across the Border for the first time after leading the North to their 1947 final win.

The late Antrim star won his third medal in that success, having been on duty in attack in the exciting squad that won the province's first interprovincial title in 1942. He helped Ulster to retain the title the following year.

LONG WAIT

Ulster had a long wait for their first win in the Railway Cup in hurling over Munster. That came at Casement Park in October 1993, when Ulster won a semi-final by 0-21 to 0-18.

Paul McKillen (Antrim) and Chris Mageean (Down) were giants in the record-making Northern team. They dominated midfield to set the scene for the winning show.

The 1993 season also saw more history for Ulster as the province made a successful defence of the football title at the expense of Leinster (1-12 to 0-12) at Longford.

Martin McHugh captained the team from centre half forward to become the first Donegal man to lead the province to an interprovincial title.

Only two counties have yet to provide an Ulster title winning team in football – Armagh and Monaghan.

POTTERTON WALKS TALL

Pat Potterton walked particularly tall in senior hurling in 1993. He was top scorer for Meath in their march to the All-Ireland "B" hurling title, and later in the year won his place in the Leinster team for the interprovincial semi-final against Connacht.

The East won that game, and Potterton retained his place in attack for the final against Ulster. He had a fine game in the Casement Park win to become the first Meath hurler to win a Railway Cup medal on the field of play.

PURCELL SUPREME

Seán Purcell, one of the outstanding figures of the 'Fifties, and rated by many as Galway's greatest footballer ever, carved out unique niches in the history of the game.

He had a thirteen year span in the Connacht team from 1949 to 1961, inclusive, a record for a Galway man. He also had the ability to do an excellent job in a variety of roles.

In 17 outings with the province, Purcell played at right half forward, centre half forward, full forward, midfield, and, amazingly enough, full back. A tremendous tribute that to his versatility and all round class.

With Connacht not having won the title since 1969, it is interesting to record that Purcell won medals in 1951 at midfield, and in 1957 and 1958 at centre half forward.

DOUBLE JOY DAY

It was a double joy day for Ollie Freaney (Dublin) and Stephen White (Louth) when Leinster completed the first sequence of four Railway Cup football titles in succession in 1955. They were the only players to figure in all eight games. Neither had to retire at any stage in any game.

The Louth man shone as a back, a midfielder and a forward over that great series.

Kevin Heffernan (Dublin), who played in all the games except the 1955 semi-final, in which he was not chosen, was Leinster's top scorer, with 5-25 (40 points), an average of 5.71 points.

RAILWAY CUP ROLL OF HONOUR
HURLING

39	Munster:	1928, 1929, 1930, 1931, 1934, 1935, 1937, 1938, 1939, 1940, 1942, 1943, 1944, 1945, 1946, 1948, 1949, 1950, 1951, 1952, 1953, 1955, 1957, 1958, 1959, 1960, 1961, 1963, 1966, 1968, 1969, 1970, 1976, 1978, 1981, 1984, 1985, 1992, 1995.
20	Leinster:	1927, 1932, 1933, 1936, 1941, 1954, 1956, 1962, 1964, 1965, 1967, 1971, 1972, 1973, 1974, 1975, 1977, 1979, 1988, 1993.
9	Connacht:	1947, 1980, 1982, 1983, 1986, 1987, 1989, 1991, 1994

Note: No competition in 1990.

FOOTBALL

23	Ulster:	1942, 1943, 1947, 1950, 1956, 1960, 1963, 1964, 1965, 1966, 1968, 1970, 1971, 1979, 1980, 1983, 1984, 1989, 1991, 1992, 1993, 1994, 1995.
22	Leinster:	1928, 1929, 1930, 1932, 1933, 1935, 1939, 1940, 1944, 1945, 1952, 1953, 1954, 1955, 1959, 1961, 1962, 1974, 1985, 1986, 1987, 1988.
13	Munster:	1927, 1931, 1941, 1946, 1948, 1949, 1972, 1975, 1976, 1977, 1978, 1981, 1982.
9	Connacht:	1934, 1936, 1937, 1938, 1951, 1957, 1958, 1967, 1969.
1	Combined Universities:	1973.

Note: No competition in 1990.

SAM MAGUIRE CUP

A FIRST ... AND A LAST FOR KILDARE!

Bill "Squires" Gannon, from Kildare Town, was the first man presented with the Sam Maguire Cup. The trophy was first awarded as the prize for the winners of the All-Ireland senior football championship for the final of 1928 and Kildare, captained by Gannon from midfield, beat Cavan by a point – 2-6 to 2-5.

That was Kildare's second successive All-Ireland senior final win, and, amazingly enough, they have not captured the national senior championship since. The success also ranks now as the last by Kildare, as that particular Sam Maguire Cup is no longer on offer for the championship.

Joe Barrett captained Kerry to victory in the second Sam Maguire Cup final in 1929, and three years later he had the distinction of becoming the first to be twice presented with the trophy.

Jim Smith brought the Cup North for the first time in 1933, following Cavan's win over Galway, and a year later the four provinces "circuit" was completed when Mick Higgins skippered Galway to victory over Dublin.

Jimmy Murray led Roscommon to their first-ever All-Ireland senior final win in 1943 and was also captain when the county retained the title the following September. He ranks as the first from the West to receive the trophy twice, and Roscommon have not won the championship since that glory era.

John Joe O'Reilly captained Cavan to victory in the only All-Ireland senior final played outside of this country. The Breffni men beat Kerry at the Polo Grounds, New York, in 1947.

Cavan retained the Sam Maguire Cup in 1948, in a decider that produced a feast of goals, by beating Mayo by 4-5 to 4-4. O'Reilly was again captain.

Seán Flanagan became the fourth man to accept the Cup for a second time after leading Mayo to their All-Ireland wins of 1950 and 1951.

Kevin Mussen walked into a special place in the annals of the Sam Maguire Cup by leading Down to their first All-Ireland final win in 1960 at the expense of Kerry. He became the first man to bring the coveted trophy across the Border.

Enda Colleran skippered Galway to their 1965 and 1966 final wins, and Tony Hanahoe earned a special place in the review in the 'Seventies.

He led Dublin to their wins over Kerry in 1976 and Armagh in 1977, and is the only Leinster man to captain two Sam Maguire Cup-winning teams.

So Near, Yet So Far

It was a case of so near, yet so far for Mick Lyons, the mighty Meath full back. He skippered the Royal County to their All-Ireland senior final win over Cork in 1987 and earned the added distinction of being the last man presented with the old Sam Maguire Cup.

A new trophy was on offer when Meath and Cork met in the 1988 final. Early that year, Joe Cassells was named Royal County captain, but he missed a number of championship games because of injury.

Because of his injury problem, he was among the substitutes for the 1988 summit, and Lyons lined out again as team leader. The match ended all square, and during the final Cassells made an appearance as a substitute.

He regained his first team position in attack for the replay, and also took over the role of captain. Meath won and Cassells earned a special place in the new Sam Maguire Cup story.

Dinny Allen led Cork from full forward to their 1989 win over Mayo to become the first Munster man to receive the new trophy.

Since then a different footballer has been annually presented with the trophy, or "Sam Óg," as many affectionately now call the Cup.

Larry Tompkins (Cork) in 1990, Paddy O'Rourke (Down), 1991, Anthony Molloy (Donegal), 1992, Henry Downey (Derry), 1993 and D.J. Kane (Down) in 1994 and John O'Leary (Dublin), 1995, complete the captain's table for the 'Nineties so far.

The Sam Maguire Cup Rankings

23	Kerry:	1929, 1930, 1931, 1932, 1937 1939, 1940, 1941, 1946, 1953, 1955, 1959, 1962, 1969, 1970, 1975, 1978, 1979, 1980, 1981, 1984, 1985, 1986.
8	Dublin:	1942, 1958, 1963, 1974, 1976, 1977, 1983, 1995.
6	Galway:	1934, 1938, 1956, 1964, 1965, 1966.
5	Cavan:	1933, 1935, 1947, 1948, 1952.
5	Down:	1960, 1961, 1968, 1991, 1994.
5	Meath:	1949, 1954, 1967, 1987, 1988.
4	Cork:	1945, 1973, 1989, 1990.
3	Mayo:	1936, 1950, 1951.
3	Offaly:	1971, 1972, 1982.
2	Roscommon:	1943, 1944.
1	Derry:	1993.
1	Donegal:	1992
1	Kildare:	1928.
1	Louth:	1957

Liam McCarthy Cup

First For McConkey

Bob McConkey was the first hurler presented with the Liam McCarthy Cup. The trophy was first awarded for the All-Ireland senior final of 1921, played in 1923, and McConkey, "the little fellow with the grey cap," as a feature in the *Irish Independent* put it, led Limerick to their win over Dublin.

Wattie Dunphy brought the Cup to the East after the 1922 final win by Kilkenny over Tipperary, and Mick Kenny led Galway to the title in the third McCarthy Cup campaign.

No Ulster hurler has yet captained a Liam McCarthy cup winning side.

Seán Óg Murphy became the first to captain two McCarthy Cup winning teams. He led Cork to their wins of 1926 and 1928, over Kilkenny and Galway, respectively.

However, the late Christy Ring earned a unique ranking in 1954 on the day he won his eighth All-Ireland medal to establish a new individual record in that regard. Ring led Cork to that win over Wexford and captained the Rebel County to the Blue Riband for the third time.

Martin Hanamy …
captained Offaly to the Liam
McCarthy Cup win of 1994

He was Leeside skipper in 1946 in a win over Kilkenny and was the team leader again in the 1953 success at the expense of Galway. The triumph a year later earned the great Cork hurler ranking as the only man to have been presented with the McCarthy Cup three times.

Mick Mackey, another legend of hurling, captained Limerick to their final wins of 1936 and 1940.

Jimmy Walsh was Kilkenny's captain in their wins of 1932 and 1939.

Nick O'Donnell, a native of Kilkenny, was captain in 1955, when Wexford won their first All-Ireland senior final in 45 seasons. He was captain again when the Model County shocked Tipperary in the 1960 summit.

ON HIS OWN

Conor Hayes has a place all his own as far as Connacht hurlers are concerned. He led Galway to their only All-Ireland senior titles double in 1987 and 1988, and ranks as the only Connacht man to have climbed the Hogan Stand steps twice to take custody of the Liam McCarthy Cup.

Jimmy Doyle, one of the greatest score-getters of all time, is another numbered in the exclusive company of hurlers who have the distinction of having captained a brace of McCarthy Cup winning teams. His big years were 1962 and 1965 with Tipperary.

HISTORY-MAKER FENNELLY

Liam Fennelly holds a number of proud distinctions in the Liam McCarthy Cup story. He captained Kilkenny to the 1983 All-Ireland final win over Cork, and that was the last year the old McCarthy Cup was presented to a Noresider.

When Kilkenny next won the title in 1992, a new trophy was on offer. Indeed the new trophy, also known as the Liam McCarthy Cup, was on offer as the prize for the winners of the final for the first time for the Kilkenny-Cork clash of 1992.

Liam Fennelly captained Kilkenny to their win, and so became the first hurler to receive the new Liam McCarthy Cup. He also, of course, ranks as the last from his county to have received the old McCarthy Cup – a rare and noteworthy double.

Eddie O'Connor captained Kilkenny in their win over Galway in the second final for the new trophy, and as a result the famed Leinster stronghold ranks as the first county to win this trophy two seasons in succession.

Back to the old McCarthy Cup, and Noel Skehan marked his All-Ireland senior final debut in 1972 by leading Kilkenny to victory over Cork. He went into that game with three All-Ireland senior medals to his credit as substitute to the legendary Kilkenny goalkeeper Ollie Walsh.

Walsh was also associated prominently with Kilkenny's successes in the new McCarthy Cup era as manager of the team that beat Cork in 1992 and Galway in 1993.

Pádraig Horan played a big part in "bringing Offaly in out of the cold" as full forward and captain in their win over Galway in 1981 that brought the Faithful County the first of their three McCarthy Cup wins.

Anthony Daly led Clare to their first Liam McCarthy Cup win in 1995. That was the Banner County's first All-Ireland senior hurling title since 1914, and only their second in all.

McCarthy Cup Winners Rankings

20	Cork:	1926, 1928, 1929, 1931, 1941, 1942, 1943, 1944, 1946, 1952, 1953, 1954, 1966, 1970, 1976, 1977, 1978, 1984, 1986, 1990.
18	Kilkenny:	1922, 1932, 1933, 1935, 1939, 1947, 1957, 1963, 1967, 1969, 1972, 1974.
15	Tipperary:	1925, 1930, 1937, 1945, 1949, 1950, 1951, 1958, 1961, 1962, 1964, 1965, 1971, 1989, 1991.
5	Limerick:	1921, 1934, 1936, 1940, 1973.
4	Galway:	1923, 1980, 1987, 1988.
4	Wexford:	1955, 1956, 1960, 1968.
3	Dublin:	1924, 1927, 1938.
3	Offaly:	1981, 1985, 1994.
2	Waterford:	1948, 1959.
1	Clare:	1995.

Outnumbered ... Conal Bonnar (Tipperary) by Dominic McMullan, left, and Olcan McFetridge of Antrim, in the 1989 Liam McCarthy Cup tie.

104

Left: Kevin Fennelly, who guarded tne net for Kilkenny in their unsuccessful All-Ireland senior hurling final bid against Galway in 1987.

Below: Michael Cleary ... won All-Ireland senior hurling medals with Tipperary in 1989 and 1991.

Below right: Kevin Heffernan ... captained Dublin to their 1958 Sam Maguire Cup win over Derry and enjoyed further All-Ireland title winning success as a Dubs team-manager

Below: Henry Downey ... brought the Sam Maguire Cup to Derry for the first time in 1993.

Players' and Officials' Index

Furlong, Martin (Offaly)   55, 80, 83

O'Donnell, Nick (Wexford) 102
O'Donoghue, Eamonn (Cork) 34
O'Donoghue, MV (Waterford) 49
O'Driscoll, John (Cork) 70
O'Driscoll, Nancy (Cork) 41, 42
O'Dwyer, Mick (Kerry) 18, 19, 28, 33, 70
O'Hara, Paddy (Antrim) 61
O'Kane, Hugh (Queen's) 61
O'Keeffe, Ciarán (St Patrick's, Cavan) 60
O'Keeffe, Dan (Kerry) 45
O'Keeffe, John (Kerry) 57, 83
O'Keeffe, R. (Laois) 49
O'Keeffe, Tony (Kerry) 62
O'Kennedy, Seán (Wexford) 7
O'Leary, John (Dublin) 11, 71
O'Leary, Peter (Kerry) 2
O'Mahoney, Dan (Mayo) 62
O'Mahony, Eoin (Cork) 86
O'Malley, Robbie (Meath) 69, 70
O'Neill, Colm (Cork) 71, 72
O'Neill, Kevin (Mayo) 79
O'Neill, Liam (Mayo) 79
O'Neill, Martin (Wexford) 45
O'Neill, Róisín (Queen's University) 39
O'Neill, Seán (Down) 61, 96
O'Reilly, John Joe (Cavan) 44, 100
Ó Riain, S. (Tipperary) 49
O'Rourke, Colm (Meath) 54
O'Rourke, Dan (Roscommon) 48, 49
O'Rourke, Paddy (Down) 4, 101
O'Rourke, Tommy (Kildare) 76
Ó Séa, Padi (Kerry) 83
O'Shea, Jack (Kerry) 54, 55, 70, 72, 80, 83, 90
O'Sullivan, Billy (Kerry) 90
O'Sullivan, Donie (Kerry) 80
O'Sullivan, Tony (Cork) 53, 60, 82, 84
Owens, Danny (Offaly) 16

Perry, Paddy (Roscommon) 75, 76
Potterton, Pat (Meath) 10, 52, 53, 98